Fr
Burgundy

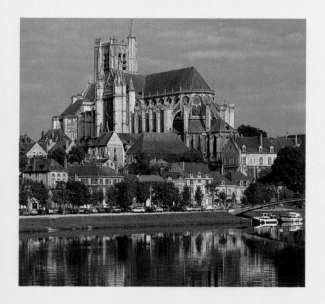

Jarrold Publishing

CONTENTS

Title page: Cathedral of St-Etienne, Auxerre

Vineyards of Meursault, Côte d'Or

Introducing Burgundy

Just try running through a list of your friends and acquaintances and consider which of them has ever been to Burgundy. There won't be many. People who visit Burgundy are – misused though the word often is – individualists. For, after doing the rounds of a handful of sights you 'really ought' to see, you must, if you are to discover the very special charm of Burgundy, find your own way quite off the beaten track.

Burgundy cannot offer beaches and guaranteed sunshine as some package-holiday destinations can. It still lacks the infrastructure to cope with mass tourism (the exceptions prove the rule). But anyone who takes the trouble to find out a little about this fascinating region can look forward to a most interesting and enjoyable holiday. Your enjoyment will be increased if you have at least a smattering of French, and access to a car. Then the lush green meadows, the wooded hills, the superb examples of Romanesque art and the delights of Burgundian wine-growing are yours to experience. Before long you will number yourself among the confirmed 'Burgundy fans' who hope that tourism never does develop too thoroughly in this unique area.

Progress and quality of life

Most tourists have an astonishingly contradictory attitude towards the idea of progress. On the one hand, when they travel in France they expect to have all modern conveniences. On the other hand, their favourite image of the French is of a chap in a beret carrying a *baguette* and cycling to the nearest café. In fact the French are justifiably proud of their technological successes, including their nuclear capability, Concorde and the TGV, the 'fastest train in the world', which thunders through Burgundy on its route between Paris and Lyon.

But when it comes to quality of life, a mixture of conservatism and shrewdness often prevails over the French love of progress. For example, if the peasants of Bresse loathe the broiler batteries of the big chicken-producers, it is because they know that a free-range chicken tastes a hundred times better than a mass-produced frozen fowl and that a Bresse chicken therefore enjoys the same sort of reputation among gourmets that a Jaguar does among motorists. And if the wine-growers of the Côte d'Or strictly limit the area of production and the permitted yield per hectare, they rightly reckon that with the high qualities achieved by such means they can further consolidate their place in the market. This is not a refusal to keep pace with the modern world but a conscious decision to continue with what they do best.

The Burgundian approach to the tourist industry is similar. Nobody has built tourist ghettos that they now regret. Burgundians have not abandoned their traditional occupations and sold their souls to the service industry of tourism. Here people have remained what they always were, farmers and wine-growers, craftsmen and small businessmen. The hoteliers, too, and the owners of restaurants and cafés have remained true to themselves: realistic, respectable, business-minded. Now, as in the past, the customers they really care for are their local or regional regulars. If people come from abroad and simply must spend their money, that's fine; but changing one's whole way of life on their account would be unthinkable. In Burgundy the tourist is not king. Here you will be treated as a guest, at best as a welcome guest. Be prepared for that.

Reading the landscape

The landscape of Burgundy is in a double sense man-made. Most people think of it as a landscape studded with art, but in a sense the art is secondary. It is above all a landscape that men have formed and fashioned. Since the Celts entered the region more than 2,500 years ago — not enough is known to speak of the situation before the Celts — numberless generations of hard-working men and women have laboured and given the landscape life. Burgundy today might have looked very different: it might have consisted of inaccessible marsh and forest instead of fertile fields, lush meadows, ingeniously terraced vineyards, orchards, market gardens, drains and artificial lakes, roads and railway lines.

But this picture of Burgundy ignores the signs of another sort of human activity through the ages: the ancient traces of the Celtic and Roman periods; the early remains of Germanic settlement and the spread of Christianity; the mighty churches and monasteries of the Middle Ages; the Renaissance palaces; the great Baroque châteaux; the little walled towns on their rocky hills; the famous wine-growing villages of the Côte d'Or; the simple hamlets everywhere. Burgundy's cloak of historic splendour glitters as though some divine hand had scattered pearls and jewels over the land. Even the plainest churches right off the beaten track gleam like gems lost in the grass. But it is the mighty basilicas of Autun and Vézelay, Tournus and Fontenay, La Charité-sur-Loire and Paray-le-Monial that are the outstanding jewels of Romanesque architecture and sculpture, which reached their artistic culmination in Burgundy.

The historic value of Burgundian civilisation does not lie merely in buildings and artefacts. We cannot imagine the religious and intellectual force with which the Cluniac and Cistercian monks brought the Christian West under their influence: it is

Cloisters, Fontenay

no longer transmitted by the remains that we can still see with our own eyes at Cluny or Cîteaux. We can learn more from literary sources of the astonishing rise to power and splendour of Burgundy in the century of the four 'Grand Dukes' than we can from the monuments in stone at Dijon. Burgundy expects that the visitor who wishes to get to know her splendid past should come prepared – and equipped with a little historical imagination.

Geographical sketch

Burgundy has always been a corridor for the great movements of population flowing through it from north to south and from east to west. It was and is a region in between. Dijon, Avallon and Auxerre belong, in the minds of their inhabitants as well as in their urban style, to the Frankish north: they are oriented towards Paris. In the Mâconnais and Charollais you come across harbingers of the south: in the architecture, in the way of life, and in the climate and flora. The watershed between the rivers that flow into the Atlantic, such as the Loire and the Seine, and those that flow into the Mediterranean, such as the Saône and the Rhône, runs straight through Burgundy.

Burgundy has never enjoyed natural frontiers. The exception is the River Saône, which, from the division of the Carolingian Empire in the 9th c., divided the French east from the German west. To the north, Burgundy merges imperceptibly with the plains of the Paris basin and Champagne. To the south, it blends into Beaujolais and the Lyonnais. The landscape is predominantly undulating, gently trimmed, dotted with woods and lakes; only in the Morvan does it rise to become mountain forest (highest peaks: Bois du Roi [Haut-Folin], 902 m, Mont Preneley, 850 m, both south-east of Château-Chinon).

Essential details in brief

Burgundy: Historic region (Duchy, Province), nowadays effectively covered by four *départements*: Côte d'Or (capital: Dijon), Yonne (capital: Auxerre), Saône-et-Loire (capital: Mâcon), Nièvre (capital: Nevers).

Area: 31,727 sq km.

Population: Roughly 1.5 million.

Largest city: Dijon, with a population of around 150,000; with suburbs, 250,000.

Agriculture: Mainly high-value, high-quality production, particularly wine and cattle (Charollais breed); also fruit-growing and sheep-breeding.

Industry: Based mainly in Le Creusot, Montchanin and Montceaux-les-Mines (heavy industry and electricals), Chalon-sur-Saône and Dijon.

St-Laurent Bridge, Mâcon, Saône-et-Loire

🔖 Signposts of history

c. 18000–14000 BC: Upper palaeolithic flint industries at Solutré.

c. 600 BC (Hallstatt D period): The Vix hoard, discovered near Châtillon-sur-Seine, with its man-sized vase of Graeco-Etruscan workmanship, provides evidence for the importation and local manufacture of prestige goods probably associated with a system of paramount and secondary chiefs.

58 BC: As a prelude to his conquest of Gaul, Julius Caesar defeats the Celtic Helvetii at Bibracte (Mont Beuvray).

52 BC: Caesar breaks the final resistance of the Gauls under Vercingetorix, who is forced to capitulate at Alesia (Alise-Ste-Reine, Mont Auxois, Côte d'Or).

First three centuries AD: Roman civilisation permeates Gaul in a peaceful manner. Autun (Augustodunum Aeduorum), named after the Emperor Augustus, was the most important township in Gaul after Lyon. Christianity was already present in Gaul from 2nd c. AD (persecution at Lyon in AD 177).

4th c. AD: Widespread conversion of Gaul to Roman Christianity after Galerius' Edict of Toleration (AD 311).

After AD 406: The German tribe of the Burgundians obtains permission from the Roman military authorities to settle on the left bank of the Rhine, later being moved into Savoy and pushing into Burgundy. From 457 the Burgundians occupy the Rhône valley down to Gap.

AD 532: The Battle of Autun. The Merovingian Franks conquer and incorporate (534) the Burgundian kingdom.

814–53: The kingdom of the Franks falls apart under Charlemagne's successors. By the Treaty of Verdun (843), among other arrangements, the Saône became the boundary between what was to become the Duchy of Burgundy, belonging to France, and what was to become the Franche-Comté (Free County) of Burgundy, for centuries subject to the German emperors.

1031: King Robert the Pious of France grants Burgundy to his second son, also called Robert, as a feudal duchy in heredity and perpetuity.

1361: With the extinction of the Capetian line, Burgundy reverts to the French Crown.

1363: King John the Good grants Burgundy in heredity and perpetuity to his son Philip, who inaugurates the Valois dynasty of the 'Grand Dukes'.

1363–1404: Philip the Bold (Philippe le Hardi).

1404–19: John the Fearless (Jean sans Peur).

1419–67: Philip the Good (Philippe le Bon).

1467–77: Charles the Bold (Charles le Téméraire). The Duchy attains its widest extent.

1477: Charles the Bold is killed at the Battle of Nancy, fighting against a coalition of hostile powers. King Louis XI takes over the French heartland of Valois Burgundy, which henceforth exists only as a province of the Kingdom of France.

1601–1789: The province regains a measure of independence thanks to the creation of a *Parlement* in Dijon and the exercise of certain rights, including regional criminal justice, by the Three Estates.

1631–1789: The Condé princes hold continuous office as governors of the province of Burgundy.

Phases of history

Gauls and Romans

The Celts settled in what is now France around the middle of the first millennium BC. Because they possessed no written tradition, our information about this period is extremely meagre, limited to archaeological finds such as that of Vix (see page 38). Roman penetration of Provence was intended first to protect Rome's ally, the Greek city of Massilia (Marseille), but from 125 BC the Romans maintained a provocative presence at Aix-en-Provence, and by 100 BC the whole of southern Gaul (Gallia Transalpina) was Roman. But Roman rule was harsh and bitterly resisted, and the fate of Gaul was not decided until Julius Caesar's governorship (58–50 BC).

Caesar's conquest resulted not from a plan, but from 'a series of brilliant improvisations'. Thanks to the disunity of the Gallic peoples, he was seriously threatened only in 52 BC, when a young prince of the Arverni, Vercingetorix, who had already defeated Caesar at Gergovia, succeeded in getting the chiefs of the Gauls to make common cause at the Aeduan hill-fort of Bibracte, setting himself at the head of the resistance movement. But in the course of the fighting, the Romans' technical skill, discipline and superior tactics gave them the upper hand. Bloodied but unbowed, Vercingetorix withdrew with the bulk of his forces into the heavily fortified town of Alesia (see page 43), which the Romans promptly surrounded. Once the Gallic relief-force failed to break the Roman lines, Vercingetorix had no alternative but to surrender. (He was executed after Caesar's Triumph in Rome in 46 BC.)

It took another year fully to pacify the new Gaul, which was divided into three provinces, Aquitania, Lugdunensis and Belgica, by the Emperor Augustus in 27 BC. Gaul thus came to enjoy the *Pax Romana*, which, though repeatedly and rudely disturbed by Germanic invasions, permitted the spread of Roman civilisation throughout Gaul, naturally including Burgundy.

Though present much earlier in the area, Christianity penetrated widely into Burgundy along with the general Christianisation of the Empire in the 4th c. AD. The practice of pagan ritual at Rome was forbidden by the Emperor Theodosius in AD 391.

Burgundians and Franks

The Burgundians (*Burgundii, Burgundiones*) were an East German people who in the late La Tène period (1st c. BC) seem to have settled in the estuaries of what is now Pomerania, between the mouths of the Oder and the Nogat. As part of the great migration of the German tribes, they gradually shifted south-westwards as far as the Upper Main. By the late 4th c. AD they had dislodged the Alamanni from the area between the Taunus mountains and the Neckar (between Frankfurt am Main and Heidelberg). In AD 406–7, when the Roman army withdrew, they crossed the Rhine. Settled on the left bank of the Rhine between Worms and Mainz, they created under their king, Gundahar (the Gunther of the *Nibelungenlied*), a small kingdom by grant of the Roman Emperor Honorius. Nor is the *Nibelungenlied*'s confrontation between the Burgundians and the Huns merely legendary. A group of Huns, who had been called in as allies by the Roman general Aetius, attacked the Burgundian kingdom in 436 and slaughtered King Gundahar along with every able-bodied man – though the traditional figure given, more than 20,000 men, is evidently much exaggerated.

The remainder of the greatly weakened tribe were then settled by Aetius in Savoy, between Geneva and Grenoble (443). From here they gradually spread westwards. Thanks to reinforcement by related peoples from over the Rhine, they very rapidly recovered a degree of strength. Bit by bit they absorbed the Roman province of Lugdunensis; but early in the 6th c. they became increasingly embroiled in the political conflicts between the Salian Franks to the north and west, and the Ostrogothic kingdom in Italy under Theodoric the Great (474–526).

In 507 the Burgundians had helped the Franks, who under Clovis had imposed themselves upon the French heartland (486), to destroy the Visigothic kingdom in south-west France. When Clovis then cast covetous eyes upon Burgundy, it was protected by Theodoric. But after the latter's death, Clovis's successors, Clothar, Childebert and Theudebert, encountered little resistance when they absorbed the Burgundian kingdom into their Frankish empire (532–4). All the same, they failed to create a state that deserved the name, until finally the empire of the Franks, including Burgundy, fell into the hands of its *major-domo* (head of the royal household) Pepin the Younger, also called the Short, who in 751 had himself elected first king of the Franks at Soissons.

Pepin's son Charlemagne (768–814) ruled the Frankish kingdom strictly, eliminating the tribal duchies and achieving a degree of centralisation. But he failed to establish his empire on a permanent footing: in 843 his three grandsons divided it once again by the Treaty of Verdun. The Saône became the frontier between the western portion of Burgundy, which became part of Charles the Bald's western kingdom, and the eastern portion awarded to the Middle Kingdom of Lothair I. Despite all later alterations due to dynastic considerations or power politics, the Saône frontier between the future Duchy of Burgundy and the future Franche-Comté of Burgundy remained an important consideration right into the early modern period. It was Louis XIV who finally succeeded in incorporating the Franche-Comté into his kingdom through the Treaty of Nijmegen (1678). (The Franche-Comté is nowadays a purely historical notion. It used to adjoin Switzerland to the east, Alsace to the north-east, Lorraine and Champagne to the north; to the west was the Saône, to the south-west and south Bresse and the Lyonnais.)

The Duchy of Burgundy

Lothair's Middle Kingdom, stretching from Bremen to the Abruzzo, harboured the seeds of its disintegration even at its inception. Immediately after his death (855), it was partitioned between his three sons. Burgundy and Provence fell to Charles, who died in 863, and his share was further divided between the two survivors. In 877 'Lower' (Cisjurane) Burgundy, centred on Provence, became an independent kingdom under Boso of Vienne (capital at Arles). In 888 'Upper' (Transjurane) Burgundy, roughly Lorraine and the Franche-Comté, became an autonomous kingdom under Rudolph I. In the breakup of the West Frankish kingdom (the bulk of modern France) after 877, 'our' Burgundy, including Autun, Langres, Troyes, Sens, Chalon and Mâcon, became the Duchy of Burgundy.

After the extinction of the line of the first dukes of Burgundy, continuous conflicts among the heirs led finally to Robert, the second son of the Capetian King of France Robert II, being awarded the Duchy 'in heredity and in perpetuity' (1031). He thus established the Capetian line in Burgundy too. Until 1361 the dukes, residing first in

Beaune, later in Dijon, descended in this line. Their power was certainly circumscribed. The region had numerous small lords who did as they pleased in their own territories and paid but little heed to the dukes. You can still see a few ruins of their feudal castles dotted about here and there.

Until the reign of Louis VI (the Fat, 1108–37), the French kings themselves also had enormous difficulties with their high-handed, mettlesome and grasping feudal lords. Law and order were of no account, and it was immensely difficult for royal authority to make headway.

The real guiding force of the period came from the religious orders; both the Cluniacs (founded 910) and the Cistercians (1098) originated in Burgundy. Their influence upon the spiritual and intellectual development of the West can scarcely be overestimated – recall, for instance, the great conflicts between the Holy Roman Emperors and the popes, in which Cistercians played the part of referee, or the Crusader movement to 'free the Holy Land' from the 'Infidel'.

The century of the 'Grand Dukes'

The line of the dukes of Burgundy, cadet branch of the Capetians, came to an end in 1361. In 1363 the Valois king of France, John the Good, bestowed the Duchy on his son Philip: once again Burgundy was awarded to a cadet branch of the French ruling family. Under the 'Grand Dukes', the *Grands Ducs d'Occident* as they were called (1363–1477), Burgundy enjoyed its golden age and played a part on the international stage. The dukes' realm extended right up to the North Sea, and in the two ducal seats of Dijon and Bruges they created a luxurious and courtly life-style.

Philip the Bold (1363–1404)

Philip earned his sobriquet when he was still almost a child. He fought the English 'like a hero' at his father's side at the Battle of Poitiers (1356), and shared his captivity in England. In recognition of his services he was granted the feudal Duchy

The sarcophagus of Philip the Bold in Dijon museum

of Burgundy when it became available. But it was he himself who laid the foundation of his power and wealth by marrying Margaret of Flanders, the 'richest heiress in Europe'. As her dowry she brought, apart from Flanders, the title to the Duchies of Artois, Nevers and the Franche-Comté of Burgundy. All these Philip acquired in 1384.

But that was just the first step. Philip worked single-mindedly to enlarge his new domains in the north. Diplomacy, pressure and dynastic marriages brought him and his successors the Duchy of Brabant-Limbourg and Hainault (1430), Zeeland and Holland (1433), Rethel (1384), the Counties of Namur (1421) and Cambrai (1435), the Duchies of Luxembourg (1451) and Geldern (1473), and the Prince-Bishoprics of Liège and Utrecht.

This accumulation of wealth and power in the heart of Europe brought about quite new political alignments. Burgundy, now a formidable sea- and trading-power, as well as a near neighbour of England, found it necessary to come to some arrangement with her. That was bound to lead to confrontation with the French Crown, the feudal lord of Burgundy, which was locked in bitter struggle with England in the Hundred Years War. Nor was that all. Philip the Bold was appointed joint guardian of the mad King Charles VI, which further destabilised the internal situation of France, since his rival was the King's brother, Louis of Orléans, who was also a guardian.

John the Fearless (1404–19)

Philip's death did not remove the rivalry, since it was not merely personal but also a matter of high politics. At bottom the sole question was: which was the dominant power in France, Orléans or Burgundy? Philip's successor, John the Fearless, stirred up feelings against Louis and in November 1407 had him murdered. But the killing solved nothing. The conflict between the *Bourguignons* and the *Orléans* (also called *Armagnacs*) grew into a civil war, even involving the popes in Avignon and Rome (this was the period of the Great Schism), and, of course, England, which gained advantage from the internal dissolution of France.

While the English took over the land, going from success to success, the Duke of Burgundy resided in Paris and left the defence of France to his opponents, the Armagnacs. In the course of an encounter with the Dauphin, later Charles VII, John was killed on the bridge over the Yonne at Montereau, apparently by the followers of the Dauphin, but against his wish.

Philip the Good (1419–67)

This murder did no more than the earlier to solve problems in France. Philip the Good pursued exactly the same policy as his father, ever concerned to protect the interests of Burgundy without appearing to betray the cause of France. In fact he was the best ally the English could have hoped for. It was Philip they had to thank for the Treaty of Troyes (1420), which is generally recognised as the most shameful agreement in French history: the Dauphin was declared guilty of the murder at Montereau and disinherited; Catherine, the Dauphin's sister, was betrothed to Henry V of England, who was to inherit the throne. The dual monarchy under English sovereignty, the ancient English dream and French nightmare, was all but a reality.

But suddenly, on August 31st 1422, Henry died, only thirty-five years old. Both kingdoms rested in the hands of incompetent kings; all the carefully laid plans were brought to nought. Shortly afterwards the mad French King Charles VI also died. But the chances of his successor, Charles VII, overcoming England and Burgundy were minimal: the 'King of Bourges' had neither money nor troops. But then the cavalry arrived: Joan of Arc, the milkmaid from Domrémy, succeeded in rousing the shattered confidence of the French and raising the English siege of Orléans. In 1429 she accompanied Charles VII to Reims, where he was anointed King.

Though the King proved not to be able to exploit his advantage to the full, and allowed Joan to be delivered by the Burgundians to the English, finally to be burned at the stake in Rouen (1431), the French Crown began to recover. And Philip the Good probably contributed his mite by shifting circumspectly from

Philip the Good

confrontation to co-operation. When the French King came to terms with the Duke of Burgundy by the Peace of Arras (1435), it was not merely the civil war that ended: the Hundred Years War also began to turn in favour of the French, until England allowed it to expire in the 1450s without a formal peace treaty.

In expiation of the murder at Montereau, Philip the Good obtained the grant of lands in central and northern France and the waiving of feudal obligations during his lifetime. He thus became the most powerful of all European leaders, not excluding the German Emperor. There was much talk of his being raised in rank: people said that he could have become king, that he had actually turned down the imperial purple.

In 1429 he founded the Order of the Golden Fleece (*Toison d'Or*), membership of which was the highest honour the Duke could bestow. The Order represented the highest élite in the land, and was probably supposed – this was never openly stated however – to generate a sort of Burgundian national feeling. The Fleece lasted longer than the state it dignified: after the collapse of Burgundy, the Habsburgs in Austria and Spain took over its regalia.

Charles the Bold (1467–77)

The name of the duke who brought about the downfall of Burgundy is the best known of all. Charles the Bold, who had already been heavily involved in running his father's domains during the latter's last years, was a man of great ability. But even the contemporary chroniclers, court annalists rather than critical observers of their master, are not very encouraging in their characterisations of him: proud, ambitious, ostentatious, hungry for fame, and given to flamboyance in dress.

What Charles especially lacked was patience and diplomacy. He thus threw away the advantages that his predecessors had accumulated. His greatest error was probably when he underestimated and, at Liège, thoroughly humiliated his opposite number on the French throne, the wily, intriguing Louis XI. Louis quietly closed the trap, and all the powers that felt threatened by Burgundy – the Emperor Frederick III, the Swiss, Duke René of Lorraine – had a hand in it. While Charles congratulated himself on having at long last succeeded (by the conquest of Lorraine, 1475) in gaining the corridor between the southern and northern parts of his dominions, his downfall was already assured. The Swiss, the spearhead of the coalition, defeated him soundly at Grandson and at Murten (1476). Charles was killed on January 5th 1477 at the Siege of Nancy, fighting against the united forces of the coalition under René of Lorraine. His body was found days later in a frozen pond, gnawed by wolves.

Aftermath

The political and cultural independence of Burgundy came to an end with the death of Charles the Bold. Thanks to the marriage of his daughter Maria to Maximilian of Austria (the son of Frederick III, later Emperor), which had been previously arranged, the dominions which owed feudal allegiance to the Holy Roman Empire (the Netherlands, Luxembourg and the Franche-Comté) and parts of French Flanders (Artois) went to the Habsburgs and remained for centuries embroiled in the history of the Holy Roman Empire, though with very different fates. The core of the old Duchy was forthwith taken over by Louis XI and turned into a province of France. The only remnants of Burgundy's independence were a regional *Parlement* and its own court of criminal justice. With the French Revolution even these institutions were swept away. Since then, Burgundy has been merely the sum of its bureaucratically defined *départements*.

Romanesque art in Burgundy

After the anxieties about the end of the world in the years before AD 1000, set in train by a too-literal interpretation of the Book of Revelation, the Christian West was able to breathe again: nothing had come to pass, the Last Judgement had been postponed. In addition the real threats from the Moors, the Normans and the Hungarians, under which the Christian world had for years laboured, seemed to have been allayed for good.

This relief, which is evident everywhere, assumed material form at the beginning of the 11th c. in a hitherto unexampled but quite unstoppable explosion of church building, inspired by faith but solidly of this world. Around 1050 Raoul Glaber, the chronicler of the abbey of St Benignus in Dijon, wrote: 'Immediately after the year 1000 it came to pass that the churches in all the world were rebuilt, in Italy and Gaul above all; and although most were still serviceable and there was no necessity, each Christian people set its heart on outdoing others in the splendour of their new building. It could have been said that the world, on casting off her old clothes, put on a pure white vestment of churches.'

Architecture

Burgundy was one of the areas in which the pious mania for building was especially marked – a classic transit corridor, where at that time many ideas could mingle and fertilise one another. Thanks to a central location, numerous towns, flourishing monasteries and plentiful local building materials, the construction boom was prosecuted in Burgundy with enormous energy. The humblest village fell prey to it

Ste-Madeleine, Vézelay

no less than the great monastery or wealthy civic church. The new sacred architecture was particularly prevalent in the south: long after Gothic had swept all before it in the north, people here continued to build in the solid Romanesque style. We can trace the development of the style in Burgundy continuously from *St-Philibert* in Tournus to *Ste-Madeleine* in Vézelay.

The masses and angles of a Romanesque building, formed from plain, sturdy shapes, are in the simplest instances assembled rather like a child's building bricks. This frame is clearly distinguished from the surrounding space, and is itself composed of volumes no less clearly separate from one another. The arcades are divided by string-courses, the volumes by bays. Nowhere are there fluid transitions to allow the divisions to appear pervious. It was believed that the component parts of a building could be separated 'without loss of blood' at their 'joints', as the great Swiss art historian Heinrich Wölfflin vividly put it.

The massiveness of Romanesque architecture, particularly in its early phases, can also be explained by the fact that the builders thought they had to make their churches defensible. This is especially clear in the sturdy, barely articulated wall of the façade of *St-Philibert* in Tournus: the effect of the west front is still that of a city gate. And even where defensibility is demonstrably not the intention, most Romanesque churches are defiantly fortress-like in appearance.

Of the elements of the Romanesque style, the most prominent is the semicircular round arch. The round arch was first used in windows and doorways, and later, in manifold variations, also in the gallery, triforium and external upper gallery. External upper galleries with recessed arcades are one of the most important devices for giving a structure obvious plasticity, along with the articulation of walls by means of socles, pilaster-strips and engaged columns; by the continuing variation of load-bearing elements, columns and piers, in the arcades; and by the use of multiple orders. You can conveniently study the development of such devices in their different phases in the village churches between Tournus and Cluny.

Glossary of Romanesque architectural terms

Apse: A semicircular termination of a church or chancel, usually with an altar. Often roofed with a half cupola and elaborately decorated. There may be more than one such termination (Fr. *absides*).

Arcade: A row of piers or columns divided by arches. When *blank* or *blind*, the spaces are filled with masonry; if *recessed*, the masonry is set back to create depth. In *intersecting arcades*, each arch overlaps another, which increases the degree of articulation.

Arcading: A row of arches used to decorate a wall.

Broken arch: An abbreviated semicircular arch composed of two segments that meet at a point (a pre-Gothic pointed arch). A characteristic feature of vaults and wall arches at *Cluny III* and many other Burgundian churches.

Capital: The stone member that caps a pier or column, immediately beneath the *abacus*, which takes the weight of the masonry above.
In Romanesque architecture, *cushion capitals* are commonest, often *scalloped* (a row of outline scallops) or *voluted* (with curled scrolls at corners).

Clerestory: A gallery with windows, especially in the nave, projecting above the roof of the aisles.

Crossing: In a cruciform church, the space where the axis of the nave or chancel crosses that of the transepts. Various permutations are possible, depending upon the relative lengths of nave, chancel and transepts.

Gallery: The arcade of a nave, chancel etc. between the ground-level arcade and the clerestory. Sometimes blank or recessed but often containing a passage. In Gothic architecture called *triforium*.

Narthex: A covered entrance-area at the west end of a church, generally with an arcade.

Order: A pair of shafts or columns and the arch between them. Orders are enumerated by counting the number of shafts or mouldings per member: for example, a two-order window or doorway has two pairs of shafts, and two mouldings over the arch.

Pilaster-strip: In Romanesque architecture, an external pilaster, without socle (plinth) or capital, generally linked by arcading. Also called a *lesene*.

Respond: A half-shaft running up the *reveal* (the inner side) of a window or archway.

Triforium: At *Cluny III* and elsewhere, a blank or recessed upper gallery of the nave, between the gallery and the clerestory.

Tympanum: A semicircular panel within an arch, typically over a door, and usually sculpted.

Upper gallery: Exterior blank or recessed arcade immediately underneath the eaves, both of the nave and of the aisle. Helps to break the wall up visually and to give it liveliness.

From T-shape to cruciform

One characteristic feature of Romanesque church building is the shift in ground-plan away from the T-shape of the Early Christian basilica to the cruciform design. This is due to the transept taking on ever greater spatial significance, until eventually there had to be double transepts in *Cluny III*. The more the transept was emphasised in relation to the nave, the more important became the tower over the crossing, whic', separated the nave from the raised chancel. The termination of the chancel (the apse), with its penumbra of additional chapels, ever more developed over time, also offered numerous possibilities for internal and external plastic decoration.

Ceilings and vaults

The most acute technical problem in Romanesque architecture was the replacement of impermanent wooden ceilings, which were also a constant fire-risk, by a solid and durable vault. An advantage was that the ceiling could be divided up into square or rectangular areas, like the walls and floor. The simplest solution, the tunnel- or barrel-vault, was introduced to France by the Romans but thereafter scarcely developed. The system with a future was the angled, quadripartite vault, the groin-vault, from which was developed the rib-vault, widespread in Romanesque architecture and dominant in Gothic. At Tournus you can see how the different types of vault were experimented with. The continuous broken tunnel-vault of *Cluny III*, however, represents the type of vault typical of Burgundian Romanesque. It is to be found in one form or another in many churches of the Mâconnais, Charollais and Brionnais.

In order to withstand the greater pressure which the vaults brought to bear on the side walls of the nave, the latter had to be strengthened with columns and piers. With the elevation on three (or four) levels — ground-floor arcade with broken (pointed) arches, gallery (triforium) and clerestory — there resulted a type of church in which, in *Paray-le-Monial*, *La Charité-sur-Loire* and many places in southern Burgundy, the influence of *Cluny III* can be discerned.

Cluny — medieval and modern

Cluny III and Fontenay

The imagination can scarcely grasp the impact of the once vast dimensions of Cluny III, now destroyed almost to the last stone: it was the largest church ever built until the new St Peter's in Rome. For Bernard of Clairvaux, the ascetic Cistercian, the church was the very embodiment of an imperial, worldly mentality, of human arrogance before the throne of God. In his view, Cluny III was so far removed from the rule of monastic simplicity that self-examination and contrition were urgently required, even in church-building. He thought that the Cistercian abbey church of Fontenay should rely for its effect on clarity of line and the puritan strength of the stone. All adornment that might distract from prayer should be avoided. The balanced, harmonious proportions do certainly moderate the starkness of the architecture, and the modern visitor finds the simple but consistent design of Fontenay a particularly fine example of Romanesque church architecture – if not quite in Bernard's sense.

Sculpture

Unlike the architecture, Romanesque sculpture seems to come out of nowhere. The sculptural tradition had perished for many centuries. In the ancient world, statues were the cultic focus of paganism, and many martyrs had been put to death because they refused to offer worship to idols – especially statues of the ruling emperor – hewn of stone. So it was only consistent that the early Christians would not tolerate statues in their churches, on the grounds that God, being of another world, could only be present in this one in the sacrament. Adoration of a three-dimensional image would, in their eyes, have been devil-worship. Early Christian sculpture, such as it is, tends to be confined to relief (sarcophagi) and to the recapitulation of pagan motifs in the context of funerary practice. Even the creation of grand churches after the Edict of Toleration in AD 311 seems not to have produced monumental sculpture.

How was it then that suddenly, at the turn of the 12th c., there sprang up not merely decorative carving (on capitals) but also monumental sculpture (on churches)? The art historian Bernhard Rupprecht explains it as follows: 'Romanesque sculpture avoided the accusation of idolatry for two reasons. First, it appeared on church buildings and therefore remained outside an art market. Secondly, though this sculpture was indeed large-scale, it was not fully three-dimensional: in theory and in fact it was carving in relief. It was precisely this fusion between architecture and relief, so typical of the Romanesque period, that stood in the way of a direct reference to the sculpture of classical art.'

This account is helpful, but it leaves open the question of the origins of the artists and their craft skills, after such a long break in the tradition. There evidently were no external influences, either artistic or technical. Some modest attempts at decorative sculpture seem to have been made during the 11th c., at *Charlieu* and *Anzy-le-Duc*. But it is extremely rare in the history of art to find such a short period between nothing, the full ripening of an artistic style and its apogee.

There is *one* explanation for this rapid development of Romanesque sculpture. Around the end of the 11th c. a mason's workshop developed at *Cluny III*, and created the first splendid sculpted capitals for Cluny itself. But its effects were felt far beyond its own site. And we have to assume that some of the sculptors of the small-scale capitals then dared to go on to bigger jobs, such as the monumental sculpture of the church front. Thanks to the elongated proportions of its figures, even non-experts can easily identify the style of the school of Cluny, widespread as it is among the Romanesque sculpture of Burgundy.

The finest and most beautiful sculpted capitals are to be found at *Autun*, *Vézelay* and *Saulieu*. These are the perfect archetypes of this art form.

The same cannot be said of Romanesque monumental sculpture. The doorway orders and tympana at Autun and Vézelay, for example, are splendid sculptures, but hardly summations. In this field, development continues with the Gothic cathedrals.

Food and drink

Burgundian cookery is French provincial cooking *par excellence*. The reputation of French cooking comes from two sources, of which the more important is the fact that housewives everywhere in France believe that no pains are to be spared to serve you a freshly prepared, nourishing and tasty meal. The second source is the excellence of the professionals, the master chefs (in trade jargon the *grands chefs*). They represent the world-wide reputation of *haute cuisine française* and they have to be continually creative and inventive. It is to their restless impulse towards innovation that we owe the intricate and often extreme creations of *la nouvelle cuisine*. And it is to the same impulse that we owe the fact that this cuisine has already become old-fashioned and is being superseded by the apotheosis of up-dated regional cooking.

Nowadays food in Burgundy is neither as lavish nor as heavy as it was eighty or even thirty years ago. But people here have departed less far than elsewhere from the robust and sturdy traditions of the past. So if you like hearty local cooking, you will always get your money's worth. Burgundy has an extraordinary natural wealth of produce. Lakes and forests (in the Morvan, for example) provide fish and wild mushrooms in considerable quantities. From Bresse, which is gastronomically to be included as part of Burgundy, come exquisite pigeons, chickens and other poultry. The Charollais and Auxois provide the world-famous beef of their dun cattle. Vegetables and fruit flourish best on the margin of the wine-growing areas, where the grapes will not ripen properly. Though there is only one notable Burgundian cheese, from Epoisses on the border between Yonne and the Côte d'Or not far from Avallon, a variety of local cheeses is to be found. And you shouldn't forget the vine-snails (*helix pomatia, hélices vigneronnes*), which the Romans loved so dearly that they put them into their own gardens to fatten them up.

One characteristic feature of Burgundian cooking is the substantial red-wine sauce, generally made with flour and butter, that accompanies many dishes: carp, eel and other coarse fish from still waters, poached eggs (*oeufs en meurette*), *bœuf bourguignon*, and, of course, *coq au vin*, which is hardly ever a true *coq au Chambertin* and correspondingly expensive. Both salt- and freshwater fish are cooked in dry white wine, most notably in a fish soup (*pochouse seurroise*) that the people of the Saône valley love to eat; and there is also a chicken dish with white-wine and cream sauce (*poulet en sauce*).

Many dishes are cooked with cream, for in Burgundy, as in many country regions, cream flows abundantly. For example, a piquant white-wine and cream sauce is served with ham fried in butter (*saupiquet des Amognes*). As an *entrée*, mushrooms with cream (*champignons à la crème*) are quite substantial. And if something is *à la Dijonnaise*, it comes with a very hearty Madeira sauce, or else with the incomparable mustard of the former ducal capital. *Fondue bourguignonne* has little in common with Swiss *fondue* except that it generally contains cheese (Gruyère and Parmesan), or less commonly beef. Whatever its origin, its association with Burgundy is of long standing.

Apart from Epoisses, the varieties of cheese (without which no meal in Burgundy is complete) are of only local significance. You may enjoy, for example, the soft *Saint-Florentin*, of which there is also a variant laced with *marc de Bourgogne*, a distilled wine brandy.

The desserts of Burgundy are distinguished not so much by special recipes as by size and weight. If only two of you are eating, you would probably do best to order two half-portions.

Wine with your meal — no problem in Burgundy? Unfortunately there *is* a problem, for if you intend to become acquainted with the *Grands* and *Premiers Crus* of the Côte d'Or on their home ground, you will have to dig deeper into your pocket than the normal holiday budget allows. But if you are happy to do so, you can drink good, fitting wine with your meals. Even the regional wines lowest on the AC scale, the humble *Cuvée maison* — a white *Aligoté* or a red wine from the *Hautes Côtes* — are more than merely drinkable in their own backyard.

The most popular aperitif is *Kir*, one fifth Cassis, four fifths Aligoté. After one's meal, there is *marc de Bourgogne*, of which good restaurants have a whole battery of bottles from which to choose.

Cheeses of Burgundy

As for gourmet restaurants, excellent, well-chosen food traditionally goes with a holiday in France. There is certainly no lack in Burgundy of good, ordinary restaurants with reasonable prices. In the second part of this Guide there is a list of recommendations. But if you wish for once to dine like a king and are prepared for the expense, then in Joigny, Saulieu, Vézelay, Avallon, Dijon, Chagny and Tournus there await you gourmet restaurants that may be classed among the very best in France. (Details may be found in the French restaurant guides — see page 94.)

Snails *à la bourguignonne*

Open a tin of vine-snails and flavour them with a dash of brandy. Boil, clean and dry the shells. Put a little snail-butter into each shell, then a snail, and fill up with more butter. Put the filled shells, open end up, into *godets* (snail-pots) or a snail-pan and put them covered into the oven, about 200°C, until the butter begins to bubble (8–9 min.).

Snail-butter (for about a dozen snails): beat 125 g butter until it is creamy. Season with pepper, nutmeg and a very little salt. Add 1 dessertspoon of finely chopped parsley, 1 finely chopped shallot and one finely pounded or crushed clove of garlic.

Wine in Burgundy

When the Romans conquered Gaul they apparently found vineyards already extended along the great rivers: the Rhône, the Saône, the Loire, the Seine and the Marne. Knowledge of viticulture evidently spread to the Gauls from the Greek colonies, such as Massilia (Marseille). Caesar reports that he encouraged wine-growing in order to attach the defeated Gauls to their own land and to introduce them to the arts of peace. The cultivation of the vine must have suffered severely during the influx of Germanic barbarians from the east. It recovered gradually at about the time of the expansion of Christianity in the 4th c. Charlemagne is known to have promoted viticulture in a decisive fashion: many new vineyards were begun during his long reign, particularly in the Rhineland and in Burgundy.

From *vin ordinaire* to great wine

We have no idea how the wine then produced tasted. As *vin ordinaire* it was drunk within a year and thus could not develop higher quality. It was the monks of the Middle Ages, and especially the Cistercians, who effected an improvement. They alone had enough labour at their disposal, and sufficient knowledge and initiative, to make the best of the wine – as it were to the greater glory of God. And they alone had the patience to keep it until it had reached the peak of its development.

In this case we actually know the site where the marvellous transformation of *vin ordinaire* into high-quality wine took place. The Abbot of Cîteaux acquired by legacy around the year 1100 a piece of poor, undeveloped land near the abbey, on the slopes of the valley of a small river, the Vouge. He created a sort of model vineyard, where his monks methodically set about improving the quality of the wine. Over the years, the abbey succeeded in extending the Vougeot vineyard by further gifts of land, and in 1336 a wall was built around it. From that time, *Clos Vougeot* (*clos* means a walled enclosure under cultivation) has been the very type of noble Burgundy.

Château Clos de Vougeot   *Grape-harvest*

Until its expropriation in the Revolution of 1789, Clos Vougeot was owned by the Cistercians. Nowadays the vineyard is in the possession of numerous smallholders. But most of the wall still stands, and enormous cellars and winepresses still testify to the industry and knowledge of the Cistercian monks (see page 51). The vineyards of Chablis, Pommard, Meursault, Aloxe-Corton, Vosne, Chambolle, etc. also began as monastic enterprises.

From fame to phylloxera

The renown of Burgundian wine gradually spread beyond its homeland. This was largely due to the efforts of the Valois dukes. In 1395 Philip the Bold sought to improve the quality of Burgundy by ordering vineyards laid to the Gamay grape to be grubbed up and replanted with the Pinot. And his acquisition of Flanders prompted the export of wine on a large scale to the Low Countries (and thence to England), a trade associated particularly with Nicholas Rolin, the Chancellor of Philip the Good. The fame of Burgundy later reached the court of Louis XIV at Versailles: Louis was prescribed the wine as a medicine by his court physician, Fagot. And in the Mâconnais the vintner Claude Brosse of Chasselas is still remembered for having sent two tuns of his best wine by ox-cart to Versailles, where they attracted the personal attention of His Majesty and ever after a welcome for the wines from the Sun King's courtiers.

The first attempts to market wines systematically came in the 18th c. First in Beaune, then in Dijon and Nuits-St-Georges, shipping firms were founded, sending representatives abroad, above all to England, and creating new markets for their high-quality wines.

But in the 19th c. there occurred two natural disasters. The first was the spread of oidium (powdery mildew), which seriously affected crops for much of the century, and the second, much worse, was the great phylloxera plague, which in twenty years destroyed the greater part of the French wine-growing industry. The vine-louse, a kind of aphid, originated in America and eventually spread via London to all the wine-growing areas of Europe. By 1880 most of the vineyards of Burgundy were destroyed. Salvation also came from America, where the native vine had long since developed an immunity to the louse. From about the turn of the century, the old European grape varieties, Cabernets, Pinots and Sauvignons, were grafted on to American or American–French rootstocks (as they still must be). But the costs of this undertaking were enormous, forcing many vine-growers out of business: between 1875 and 1929 the area of the Côte d'Or under vines shrank from 33,745 to 12,112 ha.

Soils, climate and grape varieties

The quality and character of Burgundy is affected primarily by the composition of the soil and the climate. The best conditions are to be found on the east-facing lower slopes of the *Côte d'Or*. Here the limestone and marl soil easily absorbs water and warms up rapidly. Such lime-rich soils produce a wine with plenty of bouquet, a high alcohol content and a long life-span. The soils on the higher slopes (*Hautes Côtes*) are chalkier and temperatures are a trifle lower. For that reason, just as on the heavy, clay soils of the plain to the east of the Côte d'Or, only wines of lower quality can be produced.

The climate of Burgundy is very variable. Even in summer the north is generally cooler than the south. Frosts in March and April are common, and this fact dictates the easterly or southerly direction faced by the vineyards on the Côte. Burgundy is sunny enough; its chief problems are rain and hail. The Côte, for instance, is drier than many other wine-growing areas of Burgundy, but more liable to hail. And everywhere micro-climates, influenced by extremely local conditions, are of crucial importance.

The third of the trio of factors that influence the character of the wine is grape variety. All great red wines from Burgundy are made from the *Pinot Noir* grape. The flesh and juice are colourless: the wine colour derives from the skin of the grapes. There is a much less important white variety. All the best white wines from the Côte Chalonnaise (Rully) and Mâcon (Pouilly-Fuissé) as well as from Chablis are pressed from the *Chardonnay* grape (at one time it was wrongly thought that the Chardonnay was a member of the Pinot family). The *Gamay Beaujolais* is also a specifically Burgundian grape and does particularly well on the sand and schist of the northern Beaujolais soil; about one third of the Mâconnais AC area and a significant area of the Côte Chalonnaise are under Gamay. Finally, the *Aligoté* is a white grape cultivated everywhere that the soil is not suitable for Pinot and Chardonnay. Of all vines in Burgundy, 60% are Gamay, 22% Pinot Noir, 15% Chardonnay, 5% Aligoté.

The wine industry in Burgundy

It is more difficult for wine-dealers and connoisseurs to find out about the qualities and characteristics of Burgundy wines than, for example, about those of Bordeaux. The vineyards of Burgundy are divided among around 9,700 small wine-growers and family businesses, with an average domain size of just four hectares. These domains (Fr. *domaine*) often do not have their own bottling plant and therefore have their wine bottled by a mobile unit that travels from domain to domain. Such wines are termed 'domain-bottled'. But the same domain may also sell a proportion of its wine to one of the 156 Burgundian *négociants* (wine-merchants), in order to raise cash or to dispose of poorer quality wine; a bigger institution can blend from a wider variety of sources to make a consistent product. (Some merchants are now even buying grapes and making wine themselves.) These merchants sold in 1984 the equivalent of 490 million bottles of wine (360 hectolitres), only 42% of which was *Appellation d'Origine Contrôlée* (AC).

Many smaller domains belong to one of the forty-four *Caves co-opératives*, which together are responsible for about 27% of total production. Most of this is sold to the *négociants*, who control about 72% of all Burgundian wine production. Only 28% of Burgundian wine is sold directly by domains.

The AC system is a modest attempt to control the quality of wine, and by no means a guarantee. It lays down six sets of standards, which cover the area of production, the varieties of grape allowed, the maximum yield per hectare, making the wine (especially chaptalisation, the addition of sugar), maturation and blending. Since 1974 a grower has had to choose the classification he wants for the whole of his crop in a given vineyard (*climat*) when he makes his declaration. Each domain has a notional basic yield, which can be adjusted up or down each year. There is an obvious temptation to push for ever higher limits on the production permitted from the most famous vineyards, but this rarely results in higher quality. The hierarchy of AC wines is *Grand Cru*, *Premier Cru*, *Village* or *Commune Wine*, *Generic* or *Regional Wine*.

Reading the label

When reading the label of a bottle of AC Burgundy, you should first note whether it is *domaine-* or *négociant*-bottled. In the first case, the label will list, apart from the volume, (1) where it was bottled, (2) the name of the wine, (3) its AC status, in the case of Grands and Premiers Crus especially with the vineyard (*climat* or a sub-division, *lieu-dit*) name, or the name of the village, (4) the vintage, (5) the name and address of the domain (owner). If *négociant*-bottled, the wine will bear a label that lists (1) the name of the *négociant*, (2) the name of the wine, (3) its AC status, (4) the vintage, (5) the address of the bottler or merchant. But you will often need a list of *Appellations* with you to work out precisely which class the wine falls into, since, especially in the case of Village and Generic wine, this is not made explicit.

The wine-growing districts

Burgundy's officially designated wine-growing areas are larger than the historical Burgundy, which is the one presented in this Guide. Some of the main areas are listed below.

Chablis has specialised entirely in the production of white wine. Chablis is a light wine with a good bouquet and has become internationally famous as a first-rate example of a great dry white wine.

The Côte d'Or consists of about 7,900 ha of vineyards, divided between the *Côte de Nuits* and the *Côte de Beaune*. The Côte de Nuits starts south of Dijon and comes to an end below Nuits-St-Georges. Red wine almost exclusively is produced here, the most famous names being Gevrey-Chambertin, Morey-St-Denis, Chambolle-Musigny, Vougeot, Vosne-Romanée and Nuits-St-Georges. The Côte de Beaune adjoins the Côte de Nuits to the south, and here are produced not only great red

Chablis — a world-famous white wine

wines but also the finest white wines of Burgundy (some would say of France). The great names here are Aloxe-Corton, Savigny-les-Beaune, Pommard, Volnay, Monthélie, Auxey-Duresses, St-Romain, Meursault, Puligny-Montrachet and Chassagne-Montrachet. The last three are famous for white wine.

The *Côte Chalonnaise* includes three areas, round Rully/Mercurey, Givry and Buxy/Montagny. Some fine red wines are produced in the districts of Rully, Mercurey and Givry, and good-quality whites in Montagny and Rully. There is a new *Appellation* for Aligoté at Bouzeron.

The *Mâconnais* lies between the valleys of the Saône and Grosne, stretching for 50 km from north of Tournus to below Mâcon itself, with 5,800 ha of AC production. The best wines are the Pouilly-Fuissés of Pouilly, Fuissé, Solutré, Vergisson and Chaintré, but the cheaper wines of Pouilly-Vinzelles and Pouilly-Loche are also good.

The *Beaujolais* has never historically been part of Burgundy, but geographically it is a natural extension of Burgundy's hilly landscape. Of the Beaujolais wine-growing area, 98% is under Gamay, producing middle- and lower-quality red wines. The vineyards (22,000 ha) stretch from Pruzilly in the north almost to Lyon; situation, soil and climate resemble those of the Mâconnais.

The entire wine-growing area of Burgundy embraces at present around 50,000 ha of land. The area under cultivation is being gradually reduced for the sake of improving the quality of the wine. The average annual AC production of around 1.9 million hectolitres, considerably smaller than the production of Bordeaux, constitutes only a fraction over 1.5% of total French wine-production. Only 18% of AC Burgundy is of the highest quality with an international reputation – indeed only 1% is of Grand Cru quality.

🚶 Exploring on foot and by narrowboat

If you are in search of nature in Burgundy, you are thrown almost entirely on your own resources. But that may well be exactly what you want as a counterbalance to all those tiring encounters with art and history!

It is only recently that the French have discovered the pleasures of walking. So the system of paths and signposting is patchy at best, and you need a pretty good innate sense of direction if you are to get to your destination under your own steam. Most paths are to be found in the forests of the Morvan – around Château-Chinon, on Mont Beuvray, round the Lac des Settons and near St-Brisson. *La Maison du Parc*, which houses the administration of the *Morvan National Park*, is here, and you will find some information about walks (see page 92). If you are more ambitious, you should obtain further information from the *Comité National des Sentiers de Grande Randonnée*, 92 Rue de Clignancourt, 75883 Paris.

But you can also get about in Burgundy without the tiresome need to set one foot in front of the other – on a narrowboat. The comprehensive canal system linking the Loire, the Rhône and the Seine makes this possible. The construction of the first canal, the *Canal de Briare*, linking the Loire to the Seine via the Loing (56 km), was begun by Henri IV in 1604 and completed in 1647. It was in fact the first double-width canal built in Europe. The final and most daring section dates from 1890 and is the work of Gustave Eiffel (1832–1923), the engineer who built the Eiffel Tower. It takes the water of the Seine collateral canal (a waterway running parallel to the Seine) by means of an aqueduct over the Loire to the Briare canal.

The canals were intended as waterways to transport cheaply bulk goods such as building materials and fire-wood. Nowadays, apart from the *Canal du Centre*, they are seldom used for industrial purposes. This encourages boating enthusiasts to meander along the quiet, often tree-lined waterways. There are about 1,200 km of canals and rivers in Burgundy and neighbouring areas that are available for boating holidays: *Canal de Bourgogne*, *Canal du Nivernais*, *Canal de Briare*, *Canal Latéral à la Loire*, *Canal de Roanne à Digoin* and *Canal du Centre*, besides considerable reaches of the Saône and the Yonne.

You do not need a navigation licence, but are given a short test run to get you familiar with everything when the boat is handed over. Running the boat is simplicity itself, and anyway the thing will hardly make more than three knots. Nor will the traffic regulations overburden your mental powers: basically, you drive on the right; those travelling upstream enjoy right of way; and you are not allowed to moor in the vicinity of bridges and locks.

Hints for your holiday

Art won't bite!

Burgundy is a marvellous place for a holiday. It has open spaces, harmony, beauty and tranquillity. The nervous bustle of hectic, pressurised modernity is confined to a limited number of places. You can meander by car along little empty roads and enjoy the delights of a predominantly gentle countryside. You can go for walks or drift along canals and rivers in a narrowboat. You can make friendly contact with the local inhabitants and get to know intimately wines that till now you have revered from afar.

But you cannot travel in Burgundy without encountering art. It demands your attention. It would be a pity if the rich art-treasures of Burgundy, its grand, timeless works of architecture, sculpture and painting, were taken seriously only by people hastening dutifully but joylessly from church to church, from museum to museum, ticking off what they are informed is 'important'. The quality, the beauty, and the secrets of Burgundian art are available to anyone who comes to them with eyes and mind open. The more you know about art and the more you are able to perceive connections and inter-relations, the more the objects you see will speak to you.

Eve, from the chancel of St-Lazare, Autun

Where to go and what to see

Dijon and the north

There is no sharply drawn line between the north and the south of France. But there can be no doubt that the transition occurs somewhere in Burgundy. Dijon, though, is clearly oriented towards the north, despite being as far from Le Havre as it is from Marseille. It would be wrong to jump to this conclusion just because of the course of the Seine, the source of which bubbles up not far outside the town. Historical considerations are of more significance: in the great days of the Valois dukes, the power of the mighty Duchy extended from Dijon to Flanders.

Dijon Pop. 150,000

Dijon is the only large town in Burgundy and, at least since the age of the 'Grand Dukes', the uncontested metropolis of the area. It is now the departmental capital of the Côte d'Or and still an important rail and road junction, though the routes of the A6 motorway and the TGV line between Paris and Lyon have left it rather out on a limb. But even if the city has lost some of its importance as a staging post, as a tourist attraction it is undiminished.

Dijon is a bishop's seat, a university city with its own Academy, and a mecca for theatre. Its trade is primarily in wine and mustard – Dijon mustard, of course. Since the Second World War, sunrise industries with high potential for development have settled in and around Dijon, unfortunately mostly on the southern outskirts, where the industrial parks edge ever closer to the precious vineyards. The population of Dijon and its suburbs is 250,000. For some years now the city, which used to look frightfully dingy, has been cleaning up its fine historic buildings and making them look brighter. The creation of a pedestrian precinct, with all its environmental advantages, has unfortunately produced a one-way system that is rather confusing to the visiting motorist – but you don't need a car to get to know the sights of the city centre.

The people of Dijon like their city, which, indeed, has almost everything to offer that one might want from a provincial city. Life here is agreeable and peaceful. Hence there are lots of pleasant places to eat and drink but no nightlife. After 11 pm you'll be lucky to see more than a few cinema-goers hurrying off home.

Dijon

From Roman settlement to ducal capital

The Gallo-Roman settlement of *Dibio* lay on the Augustan military road linking the Rhône (Lugdunum, Lyon) and the Rhine (Colonia Agrippina, Cologne) in the territory of the Lingones (capital: Langres). Neither in the Roman period nor in the following centuries did it make any mark on history, with the partial exception of the foundation in AD 525 of the abbey of *St Benignus*, which became the nucleus of a further settlement. It is only after 1000 that Dijon suddenly emerges out of the mists of insignificance, when King Robert the Pious, the Capetian King of France, made his second son, also named Robert, tenant-in-chief of the Duchy of Burgundy, and his capital became Dijon (1031).

Most of the town was burnt to the ground in 1137, but a larger and more 'modern' city was erected in its place. Slower but steady growth continued for two and a half centuries. After the extinction of the Capetian line in 1361, Philip the Bold, fourth son of King John the Good, was made tenant-in-chief of the Duchy in heredity and perpetuity (see page 10).

The heyday of Burgundy under the four 'Grand Dukes' was also the heyday of Dijon, their capital. From here Philip laboriously put together his extensive state around the core of the Duchy of Flanders, which he acquired by marriage. And to Dijon he and his successors brought architects, sculptors and painters from Paris and the Low Countries – only the best would do.

After the death of Charles the Bold in 1477 and the breakup of the Burgundian empire, Dijon did not slip back into the dull pages of uneventful history. The Burgundian heartland retained a measure of its special status with regard to the French Crown. The town became the seat of an independent provincial *Parlement* for Burgundy, representing the Three Estates (clergy, nobility and bourgeoisie) until the French Revolution. And it was the residence of the Governors, for nearly two hundred years members of the house of Condé. Important officials, judges and prosperous citizens set their stamp on Dijon society and, by means of their houses, on its appearance. Travellers to Dijon in the 17th and 18th c. celebrated the town's wealth, elegance and cultivated atmosphere.

As in many other French towns, the years after 1789 have left painful evidence of destruction. The new industrial age began with the construction of the railways, which made Dijon into the hub of east-central France – the station is still one of the biggest in France.

 What to see

The historic town centre is focused on the *Palais des Ducs et des Etats de Bourgogne* (Palace of the Dukes and Estates of Burgundy), which currently houses the town hall and the *Musée des Beaux-Arts* (museum and art gallery). You should certainly start your sightseeing here, however much or little time you have. You will require ideally about half a day.

Palais des Ducs et des Etats

If you view the palace from the Place de la Libération (formerly the Place Royale), it is 17th c. architecture that strikes the eye. You can scarcely fail to notice that the ethos of the *Parlement* was pretty well as feudalistic as that of the quasi-royal dukes. The architect Jules Hardouin-Mansart (1645–1708) was brought specially from Versailles to create the hemicycle with its arcades and balustrades (1686–1701). Even if

Bar Tower, Palais des Ducs

reach the *North Gallery*, was built early in the 17th c. On the stone base beside the stairs is a statue by Bouchard of Claus Sluter of Haarlem (?1340–1405/6), court sculptor to the first dukes.

From the Bar Court you can visit the *ducal kitchens*, a vast vaulted area with six fireplaces beneath gigantic chimneys. You can just imagine the whole oxen roasting on the spits! The famous ducal chapel, the *Sainte-Chapelle*, a masterpiece of early Gothic architecture in Burgundy, was pulled down after the Revolution to make way for the theatre built next to the palace. All that remains is the *chapter-house*.

On this side of the palace you will also come across the entrance to the *Musée des Beaux-Arts*. It is often claimed that this possesses the finest art collection in France outside the Louvre. That is an exaggeration. There are some splendid items, but also a great deal of merely specialist interest.

A special tip

If you are sound of wind and limb, you should try going up the *Tower of Philip the Good*, which you can easily fit in between viewing the palace and visiting the art gallery. Though there are 316 steep and narrow steps, from the very top you get a marvellous panorama of the whole town. It gives a particularly instructive view of the old city, which crowds right up to the foot of the tower round the ducal palace. There is a stylised plan to assist you in locating churches and *hôtels* (mansions) and planning the rest of your visit.

---

the dimensions are more modest, the model is royal. At any rate, the absolutist inspiration – the town kept at a distance from the palace – is unmistakable.

The palace, in a style typical of the late 17th c. – the 'Versailles manner' – with its monumental courtyard (*Cour d'honneur*) and two Baroque wings, looks out over the hemicycle. It is only when you enter the passageway leading right from the courtyard that you step into the late medieval world of the 'Grand Dukes'. The *Bar Court* is dominated visually by the *Bar Tower*, which for five years held an important prisoner, the Duke of Bar (from Bar-le-Duc in Lorraine), Count of Provence, known as 'good King René'. The splendid staircase, *Bellegarde*, by way of which you

The art gallery and museum

Hardly surprisingly, you will find here numerous paintings by Flemish, Ger-

Adoration of the Shepherds,
Musée des Beaux-Arts

man and Swiss masters of the 15th c., for the 'Grand Dukes' were eager collectors. Among the finest and most important paintings are *Melchior Broederlam's polyptych doors*, with scenes from the life of the Virgin, which he contributed to the carved high altar by *Jacques de Baerze* (c. 1400). In these is adumbrated a quite new, progressive style of painting in the process of freeing itself from medieval canons of art. The background gilding is de-emphasised, and not merely are landscape and architecture depicted but some attempt has been made to represent them in perspective. There is also a *Nativity* or *Adoration* by the *Master of Flémalle* (c. 1425), now generally identified as Robert Campin (c. 1375–1444), the teacher of Rogier van der Weyden at Tournai.

If you have not much time to spare, you should go fairly directly to the *Salle des Gardes*, where Baerze and Broederlam's remarkable *Gesamtkunstwerk* –

combining painting with sculpture in a single piece – is on display. Here you will also find the museum's two monumental treasures, the *tombs* made for *Philip the Bold* and *John the Fearless*, which originally adorned the Charterhouse of Champmol (see page 35). 'The extraordinary splendour of the sarcophagi, combining plaques of black marble, white alabaster, and gilt and polychrome decoration of the effigies of the Dukes, their insignia and the angels, conveys even now an idea of the material wealth and cultural aspirations of the House of Valois in Burgundy.' (Klaus Bussmann.)

The tomb of Philip the Bold was begun by Jean de Marville in 1385, added to and improved by the great Claus Sluter, and finally finished about 1410 by his nephew Claus de Werve. The tomb of John the Fearless and his consort Margaret of Bavaria is merely a replica of the first, made between 1443 and 1470.

The tombs and altarpieces in the Salle des Gardes are so splendid that a small masterpiece by Rogier van der Weyden is often overlooked: a minutely detailed but nevertheless quite timeless *Portrait of Philip the Good in the insignia of the Order of the Golden Fleece* (see page 12).

The Salle des Gardes actually served not merely as a guardroom but also as a banqueting hall. A great feast held here to celebrate the successful return of Charles the Bold in 1474 entered the annals of the Duchy.

You should take plenty of time to look round the Salle des Gardes. If you then have the energy and inclination, you may turn to the other rooms, containing works by masters of different countries and periods. Worth special attention are the works by Conrad Witz and Martin Schongauer, Rubens, Teniers and Frans

Place François Rude

Hals, by the Italian masters of the 16th c. and by members of the French school of Fontainebleau.

The department of *modern and contemporary art* has a surprisingly good and interesting collection. Its core is the collection of the patron of the arts Pierre Granville. Not only does it offer an exceptional insight into modern art, especially French art since 1930, but it is also a fine example of imaginative museum design and presentation.

The northern part of the Old Town

As you have perhaps already seen from the tower, everything of importance lies in close proximity. Besides, Dijon is a city in which past and present are so happily intermingled that it is scarcely possible to wander blinkered through the streets. You come out of the palace into the small, idyllic Place des Ducs,

which faces on to the Late Gothic rear façade. From here the tiny streets of the Old Town, the streets of the farriers, the basket-weavers, the coppersmiths, the glassblowers, radiate between the rows of houses – Rue des Forges, Rue Vannerie, Rue Verrerie, Rue Chaudronnerie. The old guilds are, of course, long since gone. In their place are antique-dealers, boutiques, wine-merchants, delicatessens and all sorts of other shops that make life more agreeable. Take special note of the row at nos. 8–12 in the Rue Verrerie, of the three fine *hôtels* one beside the other at nos. 35, 37 and 39 Rue Vannerie, and of the interesting early 17th c. *House of the Caryatids*, 28 Rue Chaudronnerie.

After looking round these lanes, follow the *Rue des Forges* from the Place des Ducs all the way down to the Place Fr. Rude. The street must once have been a very prestigious place to live. No. 34, the *Hôtel Chambellan*, was at the end of the 15th c. the house of a mayor of Dijon. The courtyard is prized as the finest example of Late Gothic domestic architecture in the city, and for that reason the *Syndicat d'Initiative* is now ensconced there. The house at no. 38, with its striking sculptural ornamentation on the façade, was built about 1560 by another mayor, Jean Maillard. Both no. 40, the *Hôtel Aubriot* (late 13th c. with 17th c. decoration), and no. 52, *Hôtel Morel-Sauvegrain* (mid-15th c.), are worth a closer look.

Notre-Dame in Dijon

From the Place Fr. Rude, turn north until you come to the Rue Musette. Nearby is the *covered market*. On market-days there is an amazing hub-bub here and in the adjacent streets. Follow the Rue Musette back, parallel with the Rue des Forges, till you come upon the church of *Notre-Dame*, which has a remarkable façade.

Notre-Dame and the Hôtel de Vogüé
The church of *Notre-Dame* is probably the house of God nearest, both literally and figuratively, to the people of Dijon. A typical product of 13th c, Burgundian Gothic, it protrudes from the heart of the Old Town. There are dozens of legends about it. The *recessed double arcade* of the façade, with its three rows of animal (mock) waterspouts, is unique. Nothing much can be made of the rather over-elaborate *doorway* with its 180 figures, for the wreckers of the Revolution belaboured it mercilessly with their sledge-hammers.

There are two reasons for the popularity of Notre-Dame. One is that in a chapel in the south aisle stands the *Black Madonna of Good Hope*, an 11th c. blackened statue of wood that is perhaps the oldest of its kind in France. The people of Dijon ascribe to her the ending of the Swiss occupation in 1513, as well as the withdrawal of the German occupying forces in Autumn 1944, leaving the city undamaged. Less holy but no less beloved is the *Jacquemart chiming clock*, in the right-hand tower. Philip the Bold had Jacquemart with his bell fetched from the Flemish town of Courtrai. The bell broke *en route* and had to be recast in Dijon. It thereby became, as it were, an honorary citizen of the town. People got so fond of Jacquemart that they began to be concerned about his bachelor state. So they gave him first a mate, then a son, Jacquelinet, and finally, about a century ago, a little daughter, Jacquelinette, to strike the quarter hours.

If you circle Notre-Dame to the north, you come across the fine early 17th c. *Hôtel de Vogüe*. It was the seat of the first president of the Dijon *Parlement*, a man evidently only too impressed with the gravity of his duties as a representative.

The southern quarter of the Old Town

Starting your stroll from the *Place de la Libération*, the hemicycle in front of the palace, proceed southwards down the Rue Vauban. Notice the inner courtyards of nos. 10, 12 and 21. There is also a fine series of grand houses (nos. 16, 23 and 29 – see inner courtyard) in the *Rue Amiral Roussin*. As one or two street names suggest, you are here in the old university area. Turn left from the Rue Amiral Roussin into the *Rue du Palais* along which you will come across the entrance to the *Palais de Justice*.

The Palais de Justice

The *Parlement* of Burgundy met here at one time. It will once again be clear that the image-conscious members of the *Parlement* spent money freely when it came to making an impression. You can see this immediately in the *façade*; it is evident too in the beautifully vaulted and wainscoted *Salle des pas perdus* (Saloon), which was a favourite meeting place for polite society, and in the individual *Chambers*, nowadays only rarely open to visitors as the courts sit here.

The municipal library

The library stands on the Rue de l'Ecole de Droit, in the former Jesuit College, a 16th c. building. It can only be visited on a limited basis, primarily by bona fide specialists. The chapel has been turned into the reading room. The library possesses a valuable collection of early 12th c. *manuscripts from the abbey of Cîteaux.*

On the way back to the Place de la Libération, you pass the *Musée Magnin* in the Rue des Bons-Enfants. The interior of this fine mansion of the 17th c. is still partly preserved, and it houses a collection of mainly French paintings of the 16th–19th c.

St-Michel

A little off the route of these two tours are two ecclesiastical buildings in the eastern part of the Old Town. One, *St-Etienne*, at the corner of the Place du Théâtre and Rue Vaillant, is now occupied by the Exchange and the Chamber of Commerce. The other, at the end of the Rue Vaillant, is the church of *St-Michel*. Begun towards the end of the 15th c. in Flamboyant Gothic, it was completed about 150 years later as a Renaissance building. The two richly articulated towers with unusual rotundas also date from this latter period. Worth a closer look is the *Last Judgement* by the Fleming Nicolas de la Cour in the *tympanum of the central doorway.*

Along the Rue de la Liberté to the Place Darcy

The *Rue de la Liberté*, linking the old quarter round the ducal palace to the newer part of the town, has been made into a pedestrian precinct, where the sole vehicles permitted are municipal buses. Though here and there are to be found modern stores with faceless fronts, there are still plenty of fine *half-timbered buildings* to be seen. To the west, the Rue de la Liberté ends at the *Place Darcy*, where the motor traffic once again sets the tone. In the 18th c. the *Porte Guillaume* was erected here, in place of an old city gate, as a triumphal arch in honour of one of the Condé princes.

A special tip

Mustard is Dijon's speciality. There is a shop in the Rue de la Liberté, *Moutarde Maille*, where you can buy mustard of every conceivable variety – a mustard orgy! Here you can find the answer to all your gift problems. Dijon mustard is quite extraordinarily good.

The cathedral

If you turn left just before the Place Darcy, you reach the cathedral of *St-Bénigne*, dedicated to the bishop of that name (Benignus) from Asia Minor, who is supposed to have brought Christianity to Burgundy. According to the traditional account, he was martyred and buried at Dijon during persecution under the Emperor Marcus Aurelius, which spread from Lyon in AD 177.

Several churches were erected over his grave, the last between 1280 and 1370, a typical example of Burgundian High Gothic with fine *colour-glazed roof-tiles* (which are, however, later). The most remarkable thing in St-Bénigne is the great *crypt*, which supported the rotunda of the earlier Romanesque church built by Abbot William of Volpiano (1001–18). The crypt has 86 columns, many with their original capitals, arranged in concentric circles. Adjoining it is an east-facing chapel that

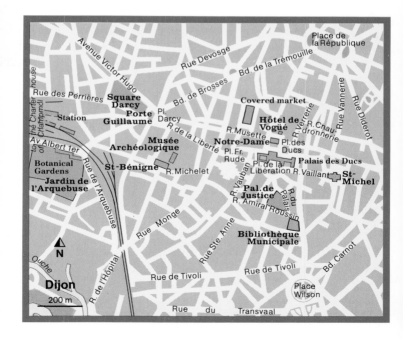

has been dated to the 6th c. On November 20th each year there is a pilgrimage to the *sarcophagus of St Bénigne*, rediscovered in excavations.

Abutting the cathedral is a building, belonging to the former abbey, which now houses the archaeological museum.

The archaeological museum

The finest section of the building is the 13th c. *dorter*, which contains some splendid late medieval sculpture (*Last Supper, Holy Family*, a *Torso of Christ* by Sluter). The Gallo-Roman finds are displayed in the basement, including astonishingly immediate reliefs showing craftsmen at work.

Now go back to the Place Darcy, where you will find all the busy activity of a large modern town – restaurants, cafés (the *Café Concorde* has the finest Parisian art nouveau interior), hotels (including the fine traditional *Hôtel de la Cloche*) and cinemas. Over the other side of the Place is the *Square Darcy*, a sort of park featuring a statue of a polar bear by Pompon. Not far to the southwest is the *Jardin de l'Arquebuse* and the *Botanical Gardens*, well known and loved for their fine old trees.

The Charterhouse of Champmol

The one attraction of Dijon that you should not try to visit on foot is tucked away in the extensive grounds of a psychiatric hospital in the western suburbs of Dijon. You reach it along the Avenue Albert I (direction N1). Philip the Bold, the first of the 'Grand Dukes', founded the Charterhouse beyond the city to serve as the burial place and chantry of the Valois dynasty. As the foundation charter expresses it, the Carthusians thus 'engaged' were to 'pray unceasingly night and day for the salvation of

Moses Fountain, the Charterhouse of Champmol

souls and for the continuing benefit of the public weal and of the princes'.

The Charterhouse was almost entirely destroyed during the French Revolution. It is impossible to gain an impression of the splendour of its former buildings. But the two great tombs and one of two altars were safely transferred to the Musée des Beaux-Arts. A great number of other items are scattered among the world's museums. On the site itself the only remnants are the *church doorway by Claus Sluter* (c. 1390) and the same sculptor's so-called *Moses Fountain*, in fact the remains of the pedestal of a gigantic open-air Calvary, partly destroyed by lightning in the 16th c. and subsequently re-erected in the monastery's covered spring. On the doorway, Duke Philip and his wife Margaret of Flanders pray on either side of the Virgin and Child. The Moses Fountain (begun 1395, completed by 1403) has five great statues of prophets standing with Christ against a hexagonal pedestal, overhung by angels. The statue of Moses, with its 'unprecedented realism', is doubtless the most impressive, and by itself makes the rather tedious trip worth while.

 De la Cloche, 14 Place Darcy; *Chapeau Rouge*, 5 Rue Michelet; *Hôtel du Nord*, Place Darcy; *Jacquemart*, 32 Rue Verrerie.

 Billoux, 14 Place Darcy; *Pré aux Clercs et Trois Faisans*, 13 Place de la Libération; *La Toison d'Or*, 18 Rue Ste-Anne (part of an old mansion, with a museum of wines); *Thibert*, 10 Place Wilson.

Ex Short excursions around Dijon

Mont Afrique (600 m), 10 km southwest: a favourite place for short excursions, with fine views.

The Suzon valley, 16 km to the northwest along the N17: a lovely leafy valley with woods all round.

The Côte de Nuits: see page 49.

To Beaune via the Ouche valley: Follow the valley up as far as Pont-de-Pany (you can take the A38 motorway, but it is more pleasant to turn off the N71 to Lantenay and reach Pont-de-Pany from there). The road (D33) is especially pretty as it goes south along the *Canal de Bourgogne* (lots of locks) and the Ouche to Bligny-sur-Ouche. From here follow the D970 to Beaune (about 70 km in all).

Famous inhabitants of Dijon

Dijon has produced several famous people, oddly enough mostly in the realm of literature. *Jacques Bénigne Bossuet* (1627–1704), theologian and pulpit orator, was famous for his funeral orations and has become a classic thanks to his standard works on history, theology and politics. *Charles de Brosses* (1709–77), jurist, historian and president of the *Parlement* of Dijon, made an entertaining contribution to the autobiographical literature of his age with his *Letters*, and wrote learned works on South Sea voyages and primitive religions. The playwright *Prosper Crébillon* (1674–1762) wrote labyrinthine melodramas that played more successfully on the susceptibilities of his own period than on those of later ones. His younger son, *Claude Prosper* (1707–77), was in his day a popular author of mildly erotic novels and stories, who married in 1740 an Englishwoman, Lady Stafford.

The sole non-literary figure is the Canon, Member of Parliament and long-serving Mayor of Dijon *Félix Kir* (1876–1968), the most popular citizen of Dijon this century. He gave his name not merely to the artificial lake to the west of the town, *Lac Kir*, but also to the drink that has since become fashionable as an aperitif all over Europe – a mixture of cassis and white wine.

The original Kir recipe

One fifth *Supercassis* (blackcurrant liqueur, at least 15% vol.), four fifths white Burgundy, more precisely *Aligoté*. You can make it with other sorts of white wine, so long as they are dry and have no strong bouquet of their own. *Kir Royal*, with champagne instead of white wine, is all very well but has nothing to do with the Canon.

North of Dijon

This is a tour round the eastern part of northern Burgundy for which you should allow two days. You will find tranquil landscape strewn with small towns, villages and fine houses; a famous abbey (Fontenay); and a splendid archaeological treasure at Châtillon-Vix.

Leave Dijon by the N71 (direction Châtillon-sur-Seine, Troyes) and pass through the Suzon valley.

St-Seine-l'Abbaye is the first stop. The eponymous saint founded a Benedictine abbey here as early as the 6th c.

The present *abbey church* (early 13th c.) marks the transition from Burgundian Romanesque to the Gothic of the Île-de-France. The façade dates from the 15th c.

After a further 8 km a little road turns left (signposted) to the source of the Seine (2 km).

The source of the Seine is tucked away in a deep, dank depression, where you can quite imagine the Celts practising their rites. The source rises in a cave embellished with a decoratively reclining lady in stone – the Celtic goddess Sequana as imagined earlier this cen-

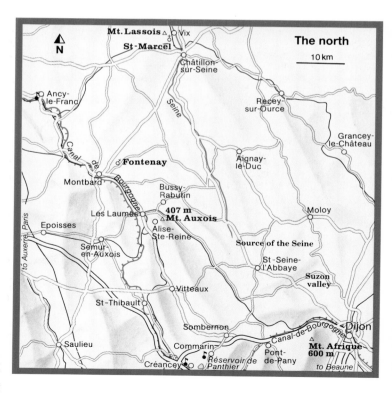

The north

10 km

tury by the *belle époque*. The spot has been acquired by the City of Paris in gratitude to the Seine for launching it on such signal prosperity.

Now back to the N71 and on, without further delay, to the next port of call.

Châtillon-sur-Seine (84 km from Dijon) has an interesting little *museum*, housed in a fine Renaissance mansion, the Maison Philandrier. It contains the *Vix treasure*, found in 1953. The Celtic settlement on Mont Lassois near Vix was inhabited in the 6th c. BC (late Hallstatt period). Excavations have brought to light more than one million potsherds, hundreds of *fibulae* (brooch-pins), weapons, ornaments and objects of daily use. The most magnificent finds came from the grave of a Celtic 'princess' who was buried half-seated in a four-wheeled cart (reconstructed).

Besides Gallic jewellery in silver and gold, Etruscan drinking cups and wine-craters (in which wine and water were mixed), some Greek vases were found. However, the most remarkable find is the gigantic bronze crater, which is 1.64 m high, 1.45 m wide and weighs 208 kg. On the rim is a frieze of warriors in four-horse chariots. The handles are in the form of gorgons, typical of the 'ori-entalising' phase in Archaic Greek art. The crater, probably of Etrusco-Greek workmanship, is one of the most important ancient finds in the whole of France.

How did the crater and the other imported goods find their way to Vix? One theory is that Vix lay on the Celtic tin route between England and the Mediterranean. At that period, the Seine may have been navigable as far as Vix, which would have been the porterage point. The Celtic lords of Vix would thus have controlled the trade in tin and levied tolls; they may also have been kept well disposed by means of diplo-

Chariot frieze on the remarkable Vix bronze crater

matic gifts. But it may also be that no special explanation of this sort is required: new excavations of sites all over France have revealed that the level of economic development of the Hall-stattian Celts, and also later in the La Tène period, was much higher than was formerly recognised, suggesting a greater degree of social stratification than had once been thought likely, and the widespread emergence of powerful local chiefs with extensive land-holdings. It is the survival of something as grand as the Vix crater that is exceptional, not necessarily its existence in Celtic France at that date.

If you are further interested in historical topography, you can push on 5 km up the N71 to Vix and *Mont Lassois*. There is nothing to see at the excavation site itself. But with a little imagination you will find yourself affected by a vision of what might have been the scene here 2,500 years ago. From the summit, on which stands the Romanesque church of *St-Marcel*, there is a fine view over the Châtillonnais.

From Châtillon, carry on along the D980 towards Montbard. Shortly before Montbard, however, turn left (sign-posted) along a little road that goes through thick woods to the Cistercian abbey of Fontenay.

Fontenay Abbey was founded in 1118 by Bernard of Clairvaux. The complex was designed as a model of strict Cistercian architecture. Building began with the church in 1130, dedicated in 1148 by Pope Eugenius III (himself a Cistercian). After the Revolution, a paper factory was created in the abbey, which was thus preserved from wilful destruction. It was restored to the condition in which you see it now at the beginning of the century by a wealthy benefactor from Lyon, assisted by some finance from the State.

Cistercian architecture is grounded upon the principles laid down by Bernard of Clairvaux: absolute simplicity and functionality. Bernard insisted that monasteries should be strictly separated from secular communities (which is still the case here) and have close by only pure running water and land fit for cultivation. They were not to accept gifts of land already under cultivation and therefore subject to feudal dues. Cistercians were to be dissociated from the stain of earthly riches. Bernard laid down the standard for this at Fontenay. It is too little known that the Cistercians' experience of farming and forestry, and especially their use of water power, were decisive contributions to the development of the medieval economy.

In spite of later alterations, the extraordinarily clear and simple use of forms, the thorough harmony and the quiet beauty of the architecture are still striking. The *cloister*, the kernel of any Cistercian abbey, is probably the most directly moving: where could one meditate better than here? But the cruciform basilican church, with its piers, broken arcade arches and transverse arches, its windowless clerestory and severe rectilinearity, is impressive in its clarity of proportion. It is not large (only 66 m long, 30 m wide at the transepts), but it

Fontenay Abbey

looks big. A gable bell-tower takes the place of a tower, which Bernard condemned as vainglorious.

Of the abbey buildings connected with the church there survive, apart from the cloister, the *chapter-house* (partly destroyed), the *scriptorium*, the *dorter* and the chafing-room, the *calefactory*, which was the only room with heating apart from the kitchen. The latter, and the refectory, formerly against the south wing of the cloister, had been demolished by 1745 in order to erect a palace for the abbot. The *infirmary* belongs to the 17th c. The visitor today is shown here a 'prison' and a *smithy*, the iron hammer of which was water-powered. It was this building that was turned into the paper factory after the Revolution.

Take pleasure in the idyllic setting of the monastery and the carefully tended park that surrounds it, but remember

Porte des Bleds, Semur-en-Auxois

that it softens the severity of the original conception. The harsh conditions in which the monks once lived can no longer be recaptured.

Montbard is only 5 km from Fontenay. The little town, which straddles the Brenne and the Canal de Bourgogne, clambers picturesquely up the Castle

Entombment group, Notre-Dame, Semur-en-Auxois

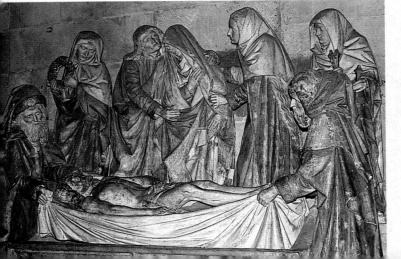

Hill: there is an attractive view from the top of the *Tour de l'Aubespin*. The former emplacements are concealed by the *Parc Buffon*, which owes its existence and its name to Georges-Louis Leclerc, Comte de Buffon. Buffon, who was born in Montbard in 1707, ranks as one of the great intellectuals of the Enlightenment. The son of a rich lawyer, he was extraordinarily versatile, a member of numerous scientific bodies but also (from 1739) administrator of the Royal Gardens in Paris. His life's work, the *Histoire Naturelle* in 44 volumes (1749–67), is a standard work of classical French literature. He wrote a good portion of the work in the little *pavillon cabinet de travail* in the park.

Semur-en-Auxois is reached by carrying on southwards down the D980 (18 km). This little town, built in the medieval period on a hill surmounted by a castle, was the most strongly fortified point in the Duchy. A citadel crowns the highest point of the ridge. Linked to it on the west is the castle. The River Armançon serves as a 'moat', since it flows round the foot of the hill, enclosing two-thirds of it. To the east, descending the hill, lies the town, itself also fortified. No wonder the place was considered impregnable.

Semur-en-Auxois with its medieval fortifications

You have the best view as you come in, from the *Pont Joly*. The car can be left in the triangular space in front of the parish church, *Notre-Dame*. Though founded in the 11th c., it dates mostly from the 13th–14th c. The north doorway (*Porte des Bleds*) is more interesting than the façade: the tympanum bears the story of doubting Thomas. Note the two snails crawling up one of the side responds: *escargots à la bourguignonne* in stone! Inside, the most arresting feature is the marvellous *ambulatory* with radial chapels.

There is a delightful walk round the *walls* on the west side of the town. For relaxing and watching the world go by, there is the tiny pedestrian precinct of the *Rue Buffon*.

Epoisses, a centre for cattle-raising and cheese-making (Epoisses is the name of the best Burgundian cheese), is worth a short detour from Semur (12 km northwest along the D954). The reason for the detour, though, is not food but the *castle*, which occupies an extensive site

Bussy-Rabutin

built up over several centuries. Its charm lies in its rather shabby state of repair: peeling paint and weeds pushing through where they evidently should not. But it would cost a fortune to restore the castle properly – certainly not to be had from the entrance fees of the few visitors who have discovered Epoisses.

Now back to Semur along the D954, which you follow through Venarey-les-Laumes and past Mont Auxois to another castle.

Bussy-Rabutin, built mainly between 1600 and 1650, is perhaps the finest pre-Revolutionary château in Burgundy. The main house, built in the style of Louis XIII between the four round towers of an older castle, is so tucked away in the well-maintained and lavishly ornamented park that you first see it when you are right upon it. But it is only when you get inside that you realise what sort of a place this is.

Roger de Rabutin, Comte de Bussy (1618–93), a gallant knight at the Court of Louis XIV, aroused the King's anger by tartly lampooning his youthful amours with Maria Mancini, Mazzarini's niece. Expelled from the Court, he wrote a satirical account of salacious Court scandals, the *Histoire amoureuse des Gaules* (1666), for which he was imprisoned in the Bastille for six years. On his release, he was again exiled to his estates, and was 64 years old before being allowed back to Versailles.

During his internal exile, Rabutin spent his time elaborately decorating the house, a pastime much to the modern visitor's advantage. He had the rooms that he spent most time in wainscoted, which made them warmer, and richly painted with fantastic landscapes and buildings, which he liked to sigh over in his isolation, with portraits of famous warriors (he was himself a brilliant soldier) and with a sort of pin-up gallery in which he amused himself with portraits of voluptuous high-bosomed ladies of the great world of the Court. And because Rabutin, besides being spirited and witty, was also malicious and vengeful (he was, you see, a first-rate courtier of the time), he inscribed mordant mottos on many of the pictures of beauties whom he had jilted or been jilted by. At Bussy-Rabutin you can learn a great deal about the shameless, but far from spiritless, age of Louis XIV and the Court at Versailles.

The park at Bussy-Rabutin is an outlier of Mont Auxois (407 m). If you sweated over Caesar's *De Bello Gallico* at school, you will recognise this mountain as *Alesia*: it was here that in 52 BC Caesar defeated the Gallic leader Vercingetorix after seven weeks of siege (see page 8). According to Caesar, the relief army that was to have raised the siege was 250,000 strong – a figure we may take with a pinch of salt.

Alise-Ste-Reine is back on your original route, a little village on the flank of Mont Auxois. From here you can drive right to the top of the mountain and park. There is a direction-finder up here, which locates the important features of the ancient and modern landscape. You can identify immediately the sites where the Romans built their camps.

High above broods the colossal *statue of Vercingetorix*, put up in 1865. Not far away (you can drive here too) are the excavations of Gallo-Roman *Alesia*, with its theatre, forum and temples – and a Frankish basilican church.

Back now to Les Laumes, where you turn left on to the D905 as far as Vitteaux (19 km). Here you may make another detour, to St-Thibault, by turning right along the D70 (11 km).

St-Thibault's once proud pilgrim church was largely destroyed by an earthquake in 1712. But you can still examine the vast ground-plan of the Gothic building, and the 13th c. *doorway* of the north transept is one of the finest in Burgundy. The sculptures of the tympanum are devoted to the Virgin Mary, those on the mouldings (only partly finished) to the parable of the wise and foolish virgins. The apse of the choir, with its elegant elevation and delicate tracery, is an astounding example of High Gothic (c. 1300). The painted high reliefs of the splendid carved altar depict scenes from the life of St Thibault (14th c.). These, and a number of other treasures, somehow escaped the Revolution.

From Vitteaux, you continue down the D905, which now passes through a particularly delightful rolling landscape. Beyond Sombernon, there is an entrance to the motorway (A38) back to Dijon. But if you like castles and grand houses, and still have time and energy, you can make yet another detour, from Sombernon to a little artificial lake, the *Réservoir de Panthier* (see map on page 37). There are three châteaux in the neighbourhood of this lake: *Commarin*, the greater part of which dates from the 18th c.; *Créancey*, converted into a house from an older fortified dwelling in the 16th c.; and finally the medieval *Châteauneuf-en-Auxois*. Partly ruined, and with its drawbridge, tower and thick defensive walls, the castle at first looks rather gloomy, but this impression is counteracted, in the inner court and the *Salle des Gardes*, by fine views over the countryside. The little village comes right up to the castle – in fact, though, it is less a village than a *pied-à-terre* in summer for the more prosperous folk of Dijon and Beaune.

Beaune

Beaune and the Côte d'Or

Beaune is one of the very finest of French towns, tiny but truly a jewel — with the one reservation that during the height of the tourist season there are times when the place is filled to bursting. To the north, west and south it is enclosed by the vineyards of the Côte d'Or. This is the true heart of Burgundy's landscape, for many the very epitome of the idea of Burgundy — just a spit of land, 40 km long by 5 to 10 km wide, but heavily populated, highly developed and intensively exploited.

Beaune Pop. 21,000

Beaune, like Dijon, has a Gallo-Roman past, though not one of any importance. From the 11th c. it was the seat of the Capetian dukes of Burgundy, who granted it fiscal and other privileges (1203). The capital was not removed to Dijon until the 14th c. and there is a slight rivalry between the two even now. But Beaune still is *the* capital of Burgundy wine.

 What to see

The town centre is the *Place de la Halle*, which is, with its big market building and the *Syndicat d'Initiative*, the obvious place for natives and tourists to congregate, whether they want to go to the Hôtel-Dieu or just to cross the road.

The Hôtel-Dieu

The ambitious parvenu Nicolas Rolin (1376–1462) succeeded in becoming adviser to John the Fearless and Philip the Good and was promoted finally to be the all-powerful Chancellor of Burgundy, in control of the entire political and diplomatic life of the Duchy. He naturally thus became immensely wealthy. Convinced in 1443 that he was on the point of death, he decided for the greater good of his soul to found a hospice for the poor. But he actually lived almost another twenty years, so that he was able to acquire for the hospice, which was anyway well endowed, vineyards in the best situations. The proceeds of the sale of the high-quality (and highly priced) *Hospices de Beaune* wines continue to finance the hospice even today. King Louis XI of France is supposed to have observed that anyone whose conscience was so burdened with the ruination of so many unfortunates was duty bound to do some good by way of compensation.

Whatever judgement we make of Chancellor Rolin's moral qualities, with the building of the Hôtel-Dieu he did make some reparation, and over the centuries many impoverished sick folk have certainly been grateful to him. But the building also serves as a monument, for himself and his wife Guigone of Salins, that could scarcely be more grand and has survived astonishingly unchanged and undamaged to the present day. Whatever Rolin was, he has left to us something very precious.

From the outside, Jacques Wiscrere's building looks plain, almost cold: a colourless façade, with hardly any articulation, and a steep-pitched roof of grey slates with a very tall ridge-turret. Only the ornamented moulding of the small doorway in the centre suggests anything special to come.

You enter the cobbled *Great Court* through a side-door and come upon a sight of overpowering splendour: 'More of a palace for a prince than a sickhouse', as was said at the time. This impression is given above all by the visual dominance of the roofs, which are lozenge-patterned in glazed Flemish-Burgundian tiles of yellow, red, black and green. The vast, plunging expanses of roof are relieved by dormers surmounted by almost light-hearted finials, which, with the warm wooden beams of the gallery, give the court an intimate air. The small ground-floor doorways, with their ogee mouldings (Fr. *arc-en-accolade*), are characteristic of Burgundian Gothic. A well with ornamental ironwork completes the 'romantic' effect. The vast *sickroom*, 52 m long and 16 m high, reminds one of a church — an impression suggested not merely by its size but also by the post-beam roof of chestnut timbers. And a sort of divine service was performed here by the compassionate nursing sisters and by the sick themselves, who were supposed to contribute to their recovery by silent prayer. The same point is made by the distribution of the twenty-eight sickbeds down each wall: the sick could see the altar in the chapel at all times.

The *chapel* adjoins the sickroom directly, separated only by a wooden rood-screen. Formerly what caught one's eye here was the great altarpiece painted by Rogier van der Weyden, the *Last Judgement*, now kept in the museum. There is one design on the chapel floor that is striking, though, and was introduced by Rolin in different forms all over the hospice, invoking *Seulle* (the One and Only), Guigone de Salins, the wife who had prevailed upon him to perform this good work. (It should be added that Guigone, herself a member of the Burgundian aristocracy, had brought as her dowry the extremely valuable saltworks at Salins in the Franche-Comté.)

The Hôtel-Dieu

The tour continues through the other rooms of the hospice ranged around the courtyard, of which the most interesting are the *kitchens* and the *pharmacy*. It concludes with the *museum*, which has been fitted up in a first-floor room which was once also a sickroom. Its great attraction nowadays is Rogier van der Weyden's great altarpiece of the *Last Judgement*. Rolin commissioned this polyptych in 1443, and it was finished in the years after 1450. The engagement of Rogier, who was born in Tournai, reflects the close artistic links between Flanders and Burgundy itself. His task was to reveal and narrate to the old and the sick in the Hôtel-Dieu a vision that would move their souls and rouse their minds from torpor – hence the array of figures of the saved and the damned. The aim of the altarpiece in its own day, of course, was more instructive than aesthetic. But it is one of the great masterpieces of the age, and is still today so well preserved that one can admire Rogier's technical control of

paint. It certainly is a pity that the altarpiece has been removed from its original position, but it does look well in the museum.

The Old Town

Next to the hospice are a number of large *wine-vaults*, where you can taste (and buy) wine. A little further on are the remains of the old *city walls*, which also have wine-vaults built into them. But if you go from the Hôtel-Dieu past the office of the *Syndicat d'Initiative* across the Place Carnot and along the Rue Carnot, you come upon the pretty *Place Monge*, where you can sit in one of the cafés and contemplate at leisure the *Beffroi*, the 14th c. curfew-tower.

As the Rue Carnot continues northwards, it becomes the Rue Lorraine. Here stand a number of Beaune's handsome 16th and 17th c. town-houses; here too is the *town hall*, formerly an Ursuline convent.

Once back at the Place de la Halle, turn left and go down the Avenue de la

République until you come to the large collegiate church of Notre-Dame (on the right).

The collegiate church of Notre-Dame, founded as a 'daughter of Cluny' in 1120, is a great mixture of medieval styles, beginning with the Romanesque apsides over the Gothic choir (13th–14th c.). The lantern above the crossing is a 16th c. afterthought. There are more attractive churches in Burgundy but the *chancel tapestries* behind the high altar outweigh that. These splendid, gloriously colourful wall-coverings of silk and linen, embroidered with scenes from the life of the Virgin (some of them apocryphal), are probably the work of the Tournai workshops in Flanders. They stand in point of style between medieval and Renaissance, which is just as it should be, since they were probably commissioned in 1474 by Cardinal Rolin, the son of Chancellor Rolin. They entered the endowment of the church in 1500.

Altarpiece by Rogier van der Weyden in the Hôtel-Dieu

The Museum of Wine

As you leave the church, there is a lane to the left that leads to the *Hôtel des Ducs de Bourgogne*, a plain but imposing 16th–17th c. half-timbered building constructed round a courtyard, as though for theatrical performances. After the dissolution of the Duchy, it belonged to the kings of France. Nowadays it houses the *Musée du Vin de Bourgogne*, which, considering that it is in the world's wine-capital, is a trifle disappointing. But the collection of winepresses on the ground-floor is impressive, and if you are prepared to go to the trouble of studying the exhibits closely, you can certainly learn a good deal about wine-growing both in general and in Burgundy.

15th c. chancel tapestry, Notre-Dame

Hôtel de la Poste, 1 Bd Clemenceau; *Hôtel Bourgogne*, Ave Général de Gaulle.

Ermitage de Corton, 4 km north on the N74 to Dijon: well appointed and expensive, but extremely good.

Wine-vaults, wine-tasting: *Caves des Cordeliers* (vaulted cellar of a 13th c. former monastery), immediately beside the *Hôtel-Dieu*; *Marché au Vins*, Rue Hôtel-Dieu; *Maison Patriarche Père & Fils*, Rue du Collège/Rue Paul Chanson; *La Reine Pédauque*, opposite Porte St-Nicolas; *Maison Calvet*, 6 Bd Perpreuil.

Les Trois Glorieuses

The culmination of the Burgundian wine year is the long weekend of the third Saturday, Sunday and Monday in November. These are called *Les Trois [Journées] Glorieuses*. The high point occurs on the Sunday, when the public auction of the Hospices de Beaune wines takes place in the Market Hall opposite the Hôtel-Dieu. Everyone who is anyone in the wine world, producer or merchant, hotelier or gastronome, is present. There is an auction of good-quality wines from the thirty-one different villages or *lieux-dits* between Aloxe-Corton and Meursault that have entered the possession of the Hospices by endowment, in some cases at the time of its original foundation.

The auction was introduced in 1850. It is an important event in the wine business, since the prices reached tend to serve as bench-marks for the other great wines of the Côte. But the steady increase in the prices paid at auction bears only an indirect relation to the quality of the Hospices de Beaune *cuvées*. It has more to do with the publicity surrounding the event and the fact that part of the sale-price goes to support the *Centre Hospitalier*, the successor to the medieval hospice.

The auction itself is quite an experience. When, by the light of the flickering candles, you see millions being paid for simple wooden barrels (full, of course), and these auctioned barrels being ceremonially sealed by their new owners, then – if not before – you begin to realise that it is wine, and not merely money, that makes the world go round. And you take your hat off to Chancellor Rolin's evident canniness, not only in founding and building his hospice five and a half centuries ago but also in setting it up on such a sound financial footing.

Many of those buying at the auction are members of the *Confrérie des Chevaliers du Tastevin*, which holds its grand annual meeting the previous evening in the *Château Vougeot* (see page 51). Guests are admitted to this as to the other meetings of the association, but must be invited – on the grounds of personal acquaintance or proven furtherance of the aims of the Brotherhood. They have nevertheless to pay a hefty 'contribution' to the costs!

The third day, the Monday, is celebrated at Meursault. A literary competition is held on the occasion of the *Paulée de Meursault*. The winner receives one hundred bottles of finest Meursault.

The Côte d'Or

What characterises the Côte is not natural beauty — the landscape is only moderately attractive — but the land itself. The highest prices for many miles around are asked and paid for land here, assuming that there is any for sale at all. The land's extreme value is due to the lime-rich plateau on whose eastern slopes the vines flourish so mightily (see page 22). The edge of this plateau extends in fact much farther than the Côte itself: it runs south for over 180 km, finally disappearing not far from Lyon.

The northern section of the Côte is named the *Côte de Nuits*, the southern one the *Côte de Beaune*. These will be dealt with in turn, starting from Dijon on the N74.

Côte de Nuits

Once you reach Perrigny, you have passed the last vestiges of the southern suburbs of Dijon. Here you turn right to Marsannay-la-Côte, where you pick up the *Route des Grands Crus*, signposted to Chambolle-Musigny. This road is narrower and more winding than the N74, but there is more to see from it.

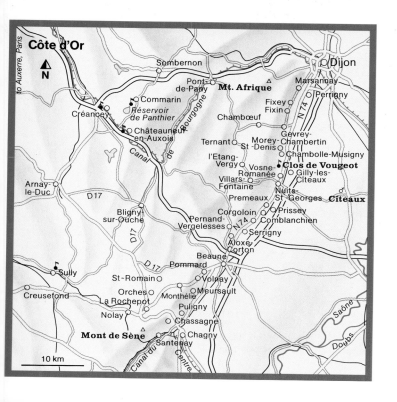

Gevrey-Chambertin

On the Route des Grands Crus

Marsannay, which is very close to Dijon, is noteworthy solely for the fact that the only *rosé* of the Côte de Nuits is produced here: otherwise red wine rules supreme. Connoisseurs rate this rosé the best in France, though much less is produced now that Marsannay has its own Appellation (since 1987).

Fixey has a little Romanesque church and is an oasis of contemplative calm amid the bustle of the vineyards.

Fixin follows immediately. It is worth mentioning less for its wines than for an odd monument to the hero-worship of Napoleon I. Whether or not you are interested in Napoleon, a visit to the little *museum* in the *Parc Noisot* behind the village really is a must. Quite apart from the usual trophies, uniforms and memorabilia, there is a sculpture, filled with pathos, of the Emperor crowned in laurel. There is a delightful and instructive view eastwards from the hill.

Gevrey-Chambertin is an imposing wine-village, given architectural weight by a medieval *castle* and a *Gothic parish church*. The latter has a fine Romanesque doorway. But the village owes its world-wide renown to *Chambertin* and *Chambertin-Clos de Bèze* (*clos* in Burgundy means a walled vineyard). These, and six other *climats*, produce the grapes for the Grands Crus, the Burgundies that are so great that the name of the village (Gevrey) does not appear on the label, only the name of the *climat* (see page 23). (Gevrey, in fact, with eight Grands Crus, has more than any other village in Burgundy.) Chambertin was Napoleon's favourite wine – though it must be admitted that as a connoisseur of wines he would not rank high on anyone's list.

 La Rôtisserie du Chambertin; Les Millésimés.

From Gevrey-Chambertin there is a worthwhile detour (c. 25 km) round the higher parts of the Côte, where extensive woodland alternates with the vineyards of the *Hautes Côtes*. The road curves round in an arc, via Combe de Lavaux, Chambœuf, Ternant, l'Etang-Vergy and Villars-Fontaine, and comes back to the Route des Grands Crus at *Nuits-St-Georges*. From here you may decide either to carry on southwards down the Côte, or to go first back along the Route as far as Vougeot, which the detour bypasses.

If you do decide against the detour, the road from Gevrey-Chambertin continues via Morey-St-Denis and Chambolle-Musigny, the *climats* of both of which produce several celebrated Grands Crus (six in all), to *Vougeot*, where the Route des Grands Crus unfortunately rejoins the main road (N74).

The Château Clos de Vougeot has, of course, long been visible. It stands proud and resplendent right in the midst of its 50 ha of vineyard. It owes its foundation to monks from the nearby monastery of Cîteaux, who began here systematically to cultivate the vine and to improve the quality of its product (see page 20).

From the outside, the château looks as though it was built in the Renaissance, which it was; but the working areas, the vaults and the *cuverie*, actually date from the very beginning, the 12th and 13th c. In the *cuverie* are four immensely large old winepresses, whose wormscrews reach right up to the roof, and about which many a fine tale is told to visitors. They are said to be the largest winepresses ever constructed.

Over the centuries, the monks of Cîteaux served the cause of winegrowing in Burgundy incomparably well. But that did not save them from being dispossessed during the Revolution. The *Clos de Vougeot* is now split up among fewer than eighty owners and produces the famous Grand Cru of the same name. But because the area is so large, it includes numerous plots that probably should not be classed as Grand Cru, especially those which extend right down to the N74, where the soil is alluvial and sometimes poorly drained. It is not merely the weather of Burgundy that makes the Grand Cru Appellations so often misleading when it comes to quality (as opposed to price).

After the Revolution the château itself had several owners until it was acquired in 1944 by the *Confrérie des Chevaliers du Tastevin*. The object of this most famous of all wine associations is to protect the quality of Burgundy and to foster and extend its reputation throughout the world (these latter efforts are prosecuted particularly in Japan and the USA). The ceremonial annual meetings (*chapitres*) are held in the vast vaults of the château – five hundred people at a time talking, eating and drinking with gusto. Visitors to the château can participate in these gatherings through the medium of a video-recording, though it provides a rather inadequate impression of the true value of the association. Among other things, at a *tastevinage* selected members blind-test, evaluate and award prizes to wines. If they select a given wine, the domain-owner or the *éleveur* who has entered it enhances his reputation and can ask better prices. The association actually guarantees the quality of the *vins tastevinés*, and in the case of complaint the bottle in question can be exchanged. There is thus a sort of quality control, and it is difficult to see how it could be much more effective without more far-reaching changes to the entire structure of the Burgundian wine industry.

Detour to Cîteaux

It seems natural at this point to go to Cîteaux, the mother house of all the Cistercian abbeys scattered throughout Europe. It lies 15 km east of Vougeot, in a rather marshy spot (*cîteaux* in Old French means a reed), which was drained and planted with trees by the Cistercians. The area has even now a rather deserted and melancholy air.

Nothing remains of the old abbey, which was founded in 1098 by Robert de Molesme as an offshoot from Cluny, and in just a few decades, under the influence of Bernard of Clairvaux (1090–1153), who entered Cîteaux in 1113, became immensely important in the history of Christendom.

The mother house was refounded in 1902 and now occupies more modern buildings dating from the 18th to 20th c. The monks do not wish to be disturbed by visitors. There is simply a slide programme on the founding of the Cistercian order and its spiritual, cultural and political significance in the Middle Ages.

You reach Cîteaux from Vougeot along a lovely, quiet little road by way of Gilly-les-Cîteaux, St-Bernard and Ville-bichot. When you get back to the N74, turn towards Vosne-Romanée.

Vosne-Romanée has some of the most famous vineyards in France, with five Grands Crus. Romanée-Conti and La Tâche have appalled many an experienced restaurant diner by being easily the most expensive wines of their vintage. If you want to gaze reverently at the Grand Cru *climats* (apart from the two mentioned above they are: Richebourg; La Romanée; Romanée-St-Vivant), they all lie north-west of the village, on the middle part of the slope, which here is cultivated to 350 m above sea-level. There is a tall cross, erected in 1804, in the Romanée-Conti *climat*.

Nuits-St-Georges

Nuits-St-Georges (pop. 5,000) is a small town just a short distance to the south. At least half its population earns a living from wine-growing or some other aspect of the wine trade. Until 1892 it was called Nuits, but then added the name of its best-known vineyard, St-Georges. It is situated more or less midway between Dijon and Beaune, and has therefore achieved some importance as a shopping centre. Together with the neighbouring community of Prémeaux, which is allowed to sell its wine under the Nuits-St-Georges label, Nuits has the largest area under vines in the entire Côte named after it, and produces the largest quantity of wine (10,747 hectolitres of red wine in 1983). It has no Grands Crus, though there are many who reckon that some of its Premiers Crus deserve to be upgraded. There is a little *archaeological museum* containing Gallo-Roman and Frankish objects found during the course of local excavations.

🛏️ *Hostellerie Gentilhommière* (motel), on the road to Meuilley, a little way out of Nuits.

Côte d'Or, 3 Rue Thurot (also has some rooms).

South of Nuits, the Côte becomes bleak and barren. The vineyards shrink, no longer dominant. Another trade takes over: the quarries of *Comblanchien* are at the heart of a flourishing industry producing a much sought-after pink-beige marble (the Paris Opéra is built of it). There are no Grands or Premiers Crus to be found here: the wines from this end of the Côte, from Prissey, Comblanchien and Corgoloin, are humbler and allowed only the name *Côte de Nuits-Villages*. They are mostly blended and thus not distinctive.

The Côte de Beaune

On the road just after Corgoloin there is a large sign announcing, just so that you know: You are now leaving the Côte de Nuits. It does not say, but you can guess, that you are now in the Côte de Beaune. And, as though it wanted to look its best for your arrival, the landscape immediately becomes more attractive, greener and more varied. As soon as you pass through Ladoix-Serrigny, turn off right to Aloxe-Corton.

Aloxe-Corton nestles beneath the *Massif de Corton* right in the middle of its vineyards. It has a small, attractive *château* with a photogenic Burgundian roof. Aloxe, with its partner villages Ladoix-Serrigny and Pernand-Vergelesses, is the only commune on the entire Côte that produces both a red and a white Grand Cru: the red is *Corton*, the white *Corton-Charlemagne*. The latter is named after Charlemagne, who is supposed to have owned a vineyard here and is reputed to have encouraged viticulture in general. There is also another white Grand Cru called Charlemagne, but, like its namesake, its fame,

alas, lies in the past.

From Aloxe-Corton you can already see the spires of the town that has given its name to this part of the Côte d'Or, the 'wine-capital' of Beaune (see pages 44ff.).

> ## A special tip
> There is a pleasant detour from Aloxe-Corton. The road is rather up and down, but that should not deter you from taking it, or from looking at the handsome domain-houses and picturesque nooks that you pass. The route lies north-west in the first instance, to the pretty wine-growing village of *Pernand-Vergelesses*, in the shadow of the hill of Corton. You will probably be tempted to drive even further north than Pernand, following the quiet roads that wind through the countryside until you end up in Nuits. All this will take you anything from half an hour to two hours. Definitely worth it!

Leaving Beaune by the N74 (direction Lyon), you shortly turn off right along the D973 towards Autun. This road leads first to Pommard and then to Volnay, both of them villages that produce splendid red Premiers Crus. Immediately after Monthélie, which may be the poor sister of Volnay with regard to wine but is extremely attractive as a village, the road turns off left to Meursault.

Meursault prides itself on producing the best white wine in the world. Such superlatives are always risky, though in the case of Meursault it may indeed be true (although plenty would claim that title for Puligny and Chassagne next door). Most people do not know that Meursault also produces some excel-

Meursault

lent red wine: that's because it is sold under the name *Volnay*. This is one of the typical inconsistencies of wine-labelling in Burgundy, a morass in which only the expert can find his or her way. But there is no question of false pretences: who may call what which name is all carefully laid down somewhere — you just can't see it on the bottle.

Meursault is a fine-looking country town with church (splendid spire), town hall, hotels and shops. The whole place looks thoroughly prosperous, the air that comes of hard, honest, profitable work. *Château Meursault*, which belongs to the Duc de Moucheron, stands on the edge of the town. Though you may not look round the house, you may visit the *vaults*, which are ancient and vast, stocked with unsuspected treasures: Grands Crus, Premiers Crus and AC wines produced by the *Domaine du Château de Meursault*, which owns valuable *climats* in Meursault itself, Vol-nay, Pommard, Beaune and Savigny-les-Beaune. Wines may be tasted and purchased at the château.

Puligny-Montrachet and Chassagne-Montrachet, the next two villages on the Côte de Beaune, are the homes of the most expensive white wines in Burgundy. The reason for their high price is not merely their quality, which is incontestable, and the length of time they need to mature, but also the tiny amounts produced (for example, only 144 hectolitres of Chevalier Montrachet in 1983). The *climat* called Le Montrachet (which means 'bald hill') really looks just like a gigantic mole-hill: it is only 8 ha in extent. The wines are more or less ordered for years ahead, which naturally pushes up the price. Two of the five Grand Cru *climats* are entirely in Puligny, one entirely in Chassagne, and two (Le Montrachet, Bâtard-Montrachet) are shared. Alexandre Dumas claimed that one should drink Montrachet on bended knee, with head bared — which only shows that wine can cause people to say the silliest things.

Santenay is the last wine village on the Côte de Beaune. It has a good deal of vineyard, but only a small yield in named wines. Most of the wine is mixed with other varieties and sold as *Côte de Beaune-Villages*. Behind Santenay is one of the highest points on the Côte, *Mont de Sène* (also known as *Montagne des Trois-Croix*, Mount of the Three Crosses). You can drive to the top, from where there is a marvellous view of the vineyards, the Dheune valley and the Canal du Centre. To the south, you can see the line of the *Côte Chalonnaise*; to the north-east, the Saône valley, with the Jura in the background. The Côte de Beaune flattens at Santenay, and the Côte as a whole thus comes to an end.

Chagny (pop. 5,000) should be mentioned here, as a little town with no sights worth speaking of, but one of the very best restaurants in France.

 Lameloise, Place d'Armes, Chagny.

Detour to La Rochepot

There are lots of little trips to be taken in the area round the Côte de Beaune, all of them worth while. If you have time, you may like to consider the following suggestions.

Take the D17 uphill westwards out of Pommard and follow the signposts to St-Romain.

St-Romain is one of those little places in the French countryside that seem at certain times of the day to be inhabited solely by women doing their knitting. But the special attraction of St-Romain is its situation. From the car-park at the end of the village, you can stroll to the rocky spur on which, of course, there once stood a castle. From here, you can look down on to the site of the new village of St-Romain, less defensible and therefore more practical, and out over the cliffs on the other side of the valley.

This is your next goal.

Drive back to the D17 and continue along it until you reach the turning to Orches (signposted) on the D171. You are now travelling (far enough from the edge to be safe) along the line of the sheer cliffs. There are a number of places where you can halt and enjoy the splendid view down the valley, to St-Romain and Meursault, right over to the Saône alluvial plain. The woods at the foot of the cliff are the haunt of nightingales. *Orches* is a little place nestling amid the rocks. From here you drive south past woods and meadows until you spy the roof of the *Château La Rochepot* to the left. Follow the signposts to the château, where there is a car-park.

Château La Rochepot stands on the site of a 12th c. castle. The substance of the present building dates from the 15th c., when the eminent Pot family lived there: Philippe Pot (1428–94), the trusty counsellor of Charles the Bold and adept survivor after the latter's death, was born in the castle. It was partly destroyed during the Revolution. When practically a ruin, it came into the

La Rochepot

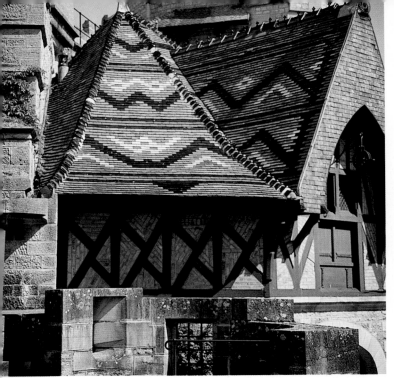

Château La Rochepot — roof detail

possession of the Carnot family towards the end of the last century. This was a period of historical nostalgia, and the Carnots restored the castle in thorough fashion. What they ended up with has been bitterly criticised by people who believe in rigorously authentic historical reconstruction: it is all too fine, too perfect to be true. But the visitor, who is unlikely to be much bothered by accuracy, will gladly fall under the spell of the lovingly recreated illusion. It is all there: a drawbridge, fountains, ramparts, watch-towers, Burgundian roofs with brightly coloured tiles, guard-rooms, chimneys, kitchens, castle chapel — a fairy-tale castle, in fact.

Below the castle lies the village of La Rochepot, on the D973. It is this road that you take to reach Nolay, which is only 4 km distant (direction Autun).

Nolay is a little town with a 14th c. *covered market* in astonishingly good condition. Take note of the solid joinery of those days.

From Nolay, you can either go back to Pommard and Beaune along the D973, or turn off right on the N6, via Puligny and Chassagne, to *Chagny*.

The trip as a whole takes at least three hours. You will enjoy it even more if you make it a whole-day excursion.

Southern Burgundy

It is usual to describe Burgundy as the link between northern and southern France. There are good reasons for this. In the days when people used notions such as race and national character less self-consciously than they do now, it was usual to speak of the two faces of Burgundy: one, with Frankish-German features, that looked to the north, and another, with Roman features, that looked to the south. Just as it is quite clear that, say, Dijon or Auxerre belong to northern France, so it is indisputable that there is already a breath of Provence in the towns and villages of southern Burgundy. The round Provençal tiles on the flat roofs are just outward signs of a difference that derives from a complex mix of geography, history and, above all, climate.

Mâcon Pop. 40,000

It is of little concern to the town of Mâcon that it is not generally known to tourists, who anyway see only the imposing house-fronts along the Saône and the traffic that swarms between them and the river. Mâcon is the capital of the department of *Saône-et-Loire*, with a fair amount of industry and a reputation as the centre of the wine trade of the Mâconnais and Beaujolais.

They say of its inhabitants that they know how to get the most out of this life. Mâcon may be thought of mainly as an overnight stop and a base for visiting southern Burgundy, but it is not without attractions of its own.

As you stroll through the *Old Town*, vivid impressions of French provincial life — relaxed, cheerful, friendly — crowd in. The best place to start walking through the narrow streets

Mâcon

View from the great rock at Solutré

is the *Quai Lamartine*. Sooner or later you will come across the finest old house in Mâcon, the *Maison de Bois* in the Place aux Herbes, a wooden Renaissance house in excellent condition, with splendidly carved decoration.

In Mâcon it is impossible to avoid encountering traces of the poet and historian Lamartine (1790–1869), who was a native of the place and spent part of his life here. Though important as a writer and politician (he was Foreign Minister in the Provisional Government in 1848), even in France he is nowadays scarcely read. For that reason, the memory of this great 19th c. figure is the more carefully cherished in Mâcon, and especially in the *Musée Lamartine*.

Other things worth seeing are the church of *Vieux St-Vincent* (Romanesque and Gothic), the *Musée des Ursulines* (prehistory, archaeology and local history), and the *Town Hall* (style of

Louis XVI) on the Quai Lamartine.

 Bellevue, 416–20 Quai Lamartine.

 Auberge Bressane, 114 Rue du 28 Juin 1944; *Au Rocher de Cancale*, 393 Quai Jean-Jaurès.

The Mâconnais

The countryside round Mâcon is very varied, but predominantly hilly. These hills often have rocky outcrops; the highest is *Signal de la Mère Boitier* (758 m). The vineyards lie on the slopes down to the Saône. The wine they produce is mostly middle-grade red (Gamay or Pinot Noir) and traded as AC Mâcon or Mâcon Supérieur. But the top-grade wines of the area are the white wines of Pouilly-Fuissé, pressed from the Chardonnay grape (indeed this grape is planted in 67% of all the 5,800 ha of AC vineyard area in the Mâconnais).

There is a *Route des Vins* from Mâcon through the Mâconnais and into the Beaujolais, but there is no need to keep to it – and it is often not signposted – in order to reach the vineyards at Pouilly. This village, with its neighbours Fuissé, Vinzelles and Loché, lies snug in a broad, sunny depression.

Solutré is the first place you reach. This wine-growing village has given its name to an entire era of the Upper Palaeolithic in France and Spain (now dated c. 18000–14000 BC). Solutrean stone implements are characteristically finely flaked, and, towards the end of the period, often worked on both sides. Excavations have established that Solutré was relatively thickly populated at that time (we are of course talking of hunter-gatherers). At the foot of the great rock of Solutré is a famous riddle, the massed skeletons of many thousands of wild horses. It is conjectured that the horses were driven on different occasions by beaters towards the cliff and then run over the edge to their deaths. But no one can say whether there were religious reasons for doing this or whether it was only to get meat to eat. Earlier still are the human skeletons from the Aurignacian period, the vast cultural complex covering the whole area from the Near East to western Europe (c. 35000–28000 BC). There are also remains from the Neolithic period (in eastern France, about 5000–2500 BC) and the Bronze Age, which suggest continuous occupation of the area with the advent of farming.

There is a car-park above the village from which you can easily climb up the rock: there's a marvellous view from the top! Solutré also boasts a small *museum*, partly built into the foot of the rock, with a good display of local prehistoric finds.

If you have time to see more than the 'important sights', it is worth driving further into the Mâconnais from Solutré along enchanting little roads. One possibility is to cross the Grosne valley and drive up as far as the *Signal de la Mère Boitier*, which again offers excellent views (a quarter of an hour's walk from the car-park). From here, via the Col de Grand Vent (D45), it is no distance to Pierreclos and Bussières. You are now on the *Circuit Lamartine*, a signposted tourist route that takes you round sites associated with Lamartine. For people who are not particularly interested in Lamartine this will be less than gripping; but the landscape is soft, with vineyards, woods, meadows filled with grazing animals and, from time to time, over to the east, views of the Saône valley. On clear days, the gentle line of the Jura mountains can also be made out.

From Bussières, the Circuit Lamartine takes you to *Milly-Lamartine*, where the writer spent his childhood and wrote some important poetry. Carefully cross the wide and busy N79, and continue to Berzé-la-Ville.

Berzé-la-Ville is a small village that is of interest because an unprepossessing 12th c. chapel stands just above it. It is on a private estate and once belonged to a priory where St Hugo of Semur, Abbot of Cluny, used to spend the summer in his old age. The inside of the chapel is covered with *frescos*, which have been described as 'among the most important and at the same time most unusual in the Romanesque art of France' (Klaus Bussmann). The dominant feature of the apse is a 4-m-high Christ in a mandorla, surrounded by the Apostles and St Paul. A parchment scroll extends from Christ's left hand to Peter, symbolising the transfer of the Law to the Church. Beneath the

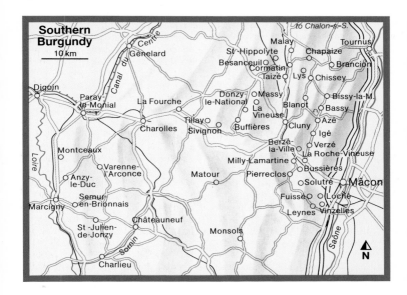

windows are groups of martyrs and saints; to the left of them, the legend of St Blasius; and to the right, the martyrdom of St Vincent or St Lawrence. They are probably to be dated to the period after the death of St Hugo in AD 1109. Art historians are particularly puzzled about the immediate sources of the obviously Byzantine forms: directly from Constantinople, from South Italy, or via the book illumination practised in Cluny?

From Berzé-la-Ville you can either drive back to Mâcon along the N79 (15 km) or push on to Cluny (12 km). If you go to Cluny, do not miss the castle that stands proud and strong, overlooking the valley.

Berzé-le-Châtel, one of the most imposing medieval castles in Burgundy, has three rings of fortifications. You can drive up to it along a narrow road. Though the inside is not open to the

public, you may look round the gardens and the terrace (with a fine view).

From Mâcon via Tournus to Cluny

This, of course, is not the direct route to Cluny, in fact it is an enormous detour.

Berzé-le-Châtel

But if your aim is to become acquainted with the best that Burgundy has to offer, then this is the road you should take.

Leave Mâcon by the N79 (westwards) and turn off right in La Roche-Vineuse to Verzé, Igé and finally Azé.

The Azé Caves are vast subterranean caverns just near the village. Remains of habitation have been found here from numerous periods, ranging from the Palaeolithic to the Middle Ages. The finds are presented in a little *museum*. The caves are open, and you can follow the course of an underground river, visit a partly reconstructed bear-cave and admire some remarkable stalactites (a round trip takes about 90 min.).

The caves of Azé are a bit of a diversion in this corner of Burgundy, which is rightly called 'the pious south': here the churches, and that means Romanesque churches almost without exception, are even more numerous than in the rest of the region. To a greater or lesser degree, all owe their existence to the powerful influence of Cluny. But moderation in all things: a surfeit of art can weigh on the spirits. And remember, the countryside constantly soothes and relieves the eye with its lush green woods and meadows, the gentle slope of the vineyards, and the idyllic roadside scenes. Moreover, these Romanesque village churches don't impose themselves, they don't insist on being visited, and they don't take revenge by prompting the anxious reflection that you may possibly have paid them too little attention.

Anyway, on you go through Bissy-la-Mâconnaise and up over the *Col de la Pistole*, where a small mountain road turns off to *Mont St-Romain*. Right on the top of the hill (579 m) is a farm run by an extremely pleasant family, who also own a small restaurant. The view from the platform of the little tower is quite overwhelming. According to the direction-finder, one can see for over 200 km, all the way to the Matterhorn and Mont Blanc. But, according to the young farmer, that is the case only very early in the morning just after sunrise, when it has just rained....

Blanot lies to the south of the Col, a neat village with a 14th c. Cluniac priory and a 12th c. church with an interesting tower. Not far away is a Frankish burial-ground.

The churches of three villages north of Mont St-Romain, *Chissey*, *Lys* and *Chapaize*, are worth looking at: the last is a particularly fine example of Romanesque architecture, with an enchanting interior and a strikingly lofty tower.

It is only 5 km from Chapaize to Cormatin, but that you will visit on the way back (see page 63). For the moment, follow the D14 eastwards to Brancion, whose walls and towers will long have been beckoning.

Brancion is a gem in a splendid setting: neither a town nor a village but a *bourg*, the French word for a cluster of houses huddled for protection beneath a medieval castle and then themselves fortified with a defensive wall (the Saxon *burh* in England is a simpler version of the same idea). It feels rather like a museum. The old houses have been carefully restored, generally by people with money who have recently bought them up. The ruined castle itself, perched on the top of the hill, has a quite magical ambience. The earliest fortification here dates to the 10th c.; the present building was erected by Philip the Bold in the late 14th c. and destroyed (1594) shortly before the end of the Huguenot war. At the other end of Brancion is the perfect little 12th c. church of *St-Pierre*, built in warm honey-coloured stone and containing frescos of about 1330. From the square in front of the church there is a magnificent view westwards over the Grosne valley and up to the highlands of the Charollais and the Morvan. If you can manage it, you should try to watch the sun set from here.

    Auberge du Vieux Brancion.

The road now wends its way down from the Mâconnais hills to Tournus, a town attractively situated on the Saône.

Tournus was in Roman times a fort on the Via Agrippina between Lugdunum (Lyon) and Augusta Treverorum (Trier). The monastery of *St-Valérien* was founded in the Merovingian (Frankish) period to the memory of St Valerian, who came as a missionary from Asia

Tournus

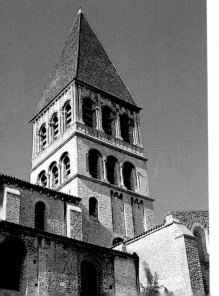

Minor and was martyred at Tournus during the persecution under Marcus Aurelius (AD 177). The monastery is supposed to lie over his grave. After the monastery of Noirmoûtier at the mouth of the Seine had been sacked by the Normans during their raids on the Atlantic coast around 840, the unfortunate monks, who had been forced to wander for years, were eventually granted the monastery at Tournus by Emperor Charles the Bald (875). They brought with them the relics of St Philibert, the founder of their monastery, who evidently had the big guns on his side: at any rate, the new abbey church, begun on a different site after 950, was dedicated to St Philibert.

The building history of the *abbey church* is fairly complicated. The first version was razed by a fire in AD 1007 but the ground-plan of the chancel, ambulatory and radial chapels was re-used in the new building. This commenced however at the west end, with the narthex; the nave was vaulted some time after 1066. The new chancel and the crossing were only finished around 1120, the three towers during the remainder of the 12th c. But the building as a whole has a splendid clarity that is even now deeply impressive. The defensive cast of the *façade* is moderated a little by the towers, which are more richly articulated. The massive, plain *narthex* also acts as undercroft to the chapel of St Michael above (an idea borrowed from the earlier church). Beyond is the *nave* with its shouldered aisles and tall drum-piers in plain masonry, which carry red- and white-striped round arches. The *chancel and apse*, with its three radial chapels, have the simplicity and formal perfection typical of Romanesque architecture at its best. The archaic forcefulness of the interior is somewhat softened by the warm pink of the stone, which comes from a quarry near Tournus. The influence of Cluny is already evident in the slightly broken (pointed) arches of the vaults in the chancel and crossing. The *crypt*, the sole survival of the church begun after 950, was dedicated by Abbot Etienne in 979 and is among the very earliest of its kind (probably based on the church of *St-Martin* at Tours). The pattern, three aisles with apsidal ambulatory and radial chapels, became canonical in Romanesque architecture. The relics of St Philibert were kept in the apse-chapel. Of the abbey buildings virtually only the north wing of the cloister survives; the chapter-house was attractively rebuilt in Gothic after a fire (c. 1240) and the municipal library now occupies the refectory and storerooms. The late 15th c. *logis abbatial* (abbot's house) stands in a small green area behind the church.

After the imperious grandeur of the architecture of St-Philibert, you can relax by strolling round Tournus. It will not take long to reach the *suspension bridge* over the Saône, which affords a fine view over the town. The *Musée Jean-Baptiste Greuze* is devoted to the eponymous painter, who was born in Tournus but most of whose paintings are in the Louvre. You will find here a few items of memorabilia, drawings, copies and portraits, and some local history – prehistoric, Gallo-Roman and medieval.

 Greuze, very close to St-Philibert.

You should now return along the D14 through Chapaize to Cormatin in the Grosne valley.

The Château de Cormatin is one of the most impressive and unified Renaissance buildings in Burgundy (1600–08).

The rooms, which are extremely richly decorated in the manner of Louis XIII, are splendid evidence of the degree of accomplishment in the decorative arts at this period: everything, paintwork, carving, joinery, tapestries, gilding and furniture, is of the highest quality. Of particular note are the *Gilt Saloon* on the first floor, the *King's Saloon* and the *Marquise's Room*. Visitors are conducted round the house in small groups by a guide. Admission to the *park* is by ticket only.

From Cormatin, there are two ways of getting to Cluny. The first is by way of the *Circuit des Églises Romanes du Mâconnais*, a circuitous route that will take you there by way of Malay, St-Hippolyte, Besanceuil, Massy and La Vineuse (about 35 km). The second is the direct road, which is followed here so that you can take in Taizé (13 km on the D981).

Taizé has become famous thanks to the ecumenical community (*Communauté de Taizé*) founded by Brother Roger (Schütz) of Lausanne in 1944. It includes eighty members from different (mainly Protestant) denominations joining in the name of ecumenism. This movement of reunification has evoked a large and enduring response, especially from young people all over Europe. Since 1960 Taizé has been a meeting point for young people who come here in their thousands to find their way to Christ in talk, worship and meditation and thus give meaning to their lives. In August of each year a Youth Council is held, which attracts around 40,000 young people. The community is not a closed order, and is open to all in search of love and reconciliation.

The modern concrete *Eglise de la Réconciliation* was erected in 1962 by the community. Since then, it has had to be enlarged in order to hold the numbers wishing to attend. The tiny, dark Romanesque parish church of *Ste-Marie-Madeleine* provides the community with a place for silent worship.

From Taizé it is now only 10 km to Cluny, where nigh on 1100 years ago a different Christian movement was born.

Cluny

The tourist's ability to conjure up the past is nowhere in Burgundy more needful than at Cluny. What you can actually see here is just a faint glimmer, a shattered body in stone, all that remains of a mighty spiritual force that radiated out over the Christian West and stamped its mark, theologically, culturally and politically, upon an entire period of the Middle Ages. There is nothing here to feel, nothing to intuit. If you are not to be terribly disappointed, you will have to do some homework.

Cluny

Rise and fall

The *abbey of Cluny* was founded on September 11th 910 by William the Pious, Duke of Aquitaine, and Abbot Berno of Baume. The purpose was to reform the Benedictine order: to restore the old rules that had fallen into neglect over the centuries. These principles were: continence, obedience, fasting, a worthy and impressive celebration of the Mass and exclusion from the monastery of all secular and, as far as possible, episcopal influence. It was therefore arranged that the abbey should be directly subject to the Pope and that other monasteries should be subject to it.

A strictly organised hierarchical system was established, whereby the abbot of Cluny became in practice the overlord of all the daughter houses. Already by the beginning of the 12th c. Cluny controlled over 1,450 monasteries and more than 100,000 monks, mostly in Britain, but also in Germany, Spain, Italy, Switzerland and Poland. The rapid expansion of the reforming spirit and influence of Cluny was also partly due to the accident that from the mid-10th c. there were only five abbots in two centuries, all of them important: Mayeul (c. 963–94); Odilo (994–1048/9); Hugo (1049–1109); Pons de Megueil (1109–22); Peter the Venerable (1122–56).

Almost necessarily, and to begin with certainly unwillingly, this extraordinary efflorescence was followed by a shift from spiritual towards secular influence. The abbots of Cluny became involved in the political conflicts of the day, advisers to the German emperor, arbitrators in the investiture dispute between pope and emperor (1075 to the Concordat of Worms in 1122) – occasionally more influential and more 'powerful' than either. 'Cluny became the driving force behind the crusades in the Holy Land and the Reconquista in Spain. Its spiritual and its secular power grew simultaneously, the one enhancing the other. Its wealth and influence were beyond reckoning.' (Wolfgang Braunfels.)

Decline, decadence and loss of influence began at latest around 1150. Decades earlier, Bernard of Clairvaux had distanced himself from Cluny: for him, it had become too worldly, complacent and self-centred. But it remained wealthy, becoming a source of desirable prebends and benefices for well-born gentlemen who rarely and with regret quit the Court at Paris. In the 18th c. the medieval monastery was replaced by a modern building which still stands. By the time of the Revolution, Cluny was a byword for the corruption of Church and nobility: the place was pillaged by the mob in 1790. From 1806 to 1823 a speculative builder from Mâcon leased the shell of the abbey and, with the aid of gunpowder, made such excellent use of his extractive rights that barely one tenth of the church, as it was in 1150, now exists.

The architectural history of Cluny has been an inexhaustible subject for PhD dissertations in art history. The first recorded church (*Cluny I*) was dedicated in 927. A second, larger church (*Cluny II*) had already been begun c. 950 and dedicated as early as 981. Within a hundred years this too had become insufficient for the needs of the now unique status of the abbey. The fame of the monastery in the Grosne valley had by now spread all over the western world. Pope Urban II (1042–99), himself a Cluniac monk, called the mother house of his order 'la lumière du monde', the light of the world. The great Abbot Hugo planned the construction of a new church whose splendour was to outdo anything the Christian world had yet seen.

Finance was not a problem. Under Abbot Hugo, Cluny had put the King of Castile in its debt for practical help with the reconquest of Spain from the Moors. Moreover, both the German Emperor (Henry IV) and the King of England (William Rufus) promised financial assistance for the massive undertaking. The foundation stone of the *abbey church of St Peter and St Paul* (*Cluny III*) was laid in 1088. It was dedicated in 1130 by Pope Innocent III in person.

One should think of the vast abbey church as a sort of *Summa Theologica* of its day in stone. It was to be 'a reflection of Cluny's wealth as well as connoting its spirituality, its essence, its yearning for expression in formal terms' (Braunfels). Only models and reconstructed elevations, such as those in the *abbey museum* and the *Musée Ochier*, can now give some idea of its hitherto unprecedented size. It was 178 m in length, longer than any other Christian building prior to the construction of St Peter's, Rome, which exceeds it by a mere 8 m. Such size was to be a symbol of the Cluniac claim to precedence in the West. The relation between the width and the height of the nave (12 : 30 m, or 1 : 2.5) must have had an astonishing impact at the time, and was only equalled again by the great Gothic cathedrals of the Île-de-France.

The narthex had two aisles (5 bays), the nave four (11 bays); the piers were composite; the two transepts each had a vaulted crossing: all of this must have had an overwhelming impact. And high above the church there arose a cluster of towers, seven in all, symbolising the greatness of God and the splendour of the heavenly city, Jerusalem.

The remnants of former glory
The sole remnants of the medieval
church are sections of the two southern
transepts and two towers, the solid,
octagonal *Clocher de l'Eau Bénite* and
its lesser fellow, the *Clocher de l'Horloge* (clock-tower). The *façade du Pape
Gélase* (the façade of the monastery),
overlooking the Place de l'Abbaye, was
built on to the complex in the late 13th
c.; and the *Bourbon Chapel* was built
into the rear transept in the late 15th c.,
of course in Gothic style.

Apart from that, the only original
remains to be seen are in the *Musée du
Farinier*, opened in 1949 in the former
granary of the abbey mill. On the first
floor you can inspect the *capitals of the
chancel*, insofar as they could be res-
cued by the city authorities in 1823.
With these capitals, so it is said, came,
virtually out of nothing, the onset of
Burgundian – indeed French – medieval sculpture, which reached its first
flowering in the tympana and sculpted
capitals at Saulieu, Autun and Vézelay.
Apart from *scenes from Genesis*
(temptation of Adam and Eve; the
sacrifice of Isaac), you should note
particularly the representations of
the *eight tones in music*, since they
hint at the central role that Gregorian
chant played in the Cluniac liturgy.
This room also contains a model of the
abbey.

The *Musée Ochier*, in the medieval
palace of Abbot Jean de Bourbon at the
end of the Rue Conant, houses some
other fragmentary remains of *Cluny III*,
especially those from the main doorway, and the narthex capitals. There are
also some interesting façades from old
12th and 13th c. town-houses, the *mai-
sons romanes*. The *Hôtel de Ville* (the
town hall) occupies another abbot's palace, built in the style of the Italian

Renaissance about 1500 by Jacques
and Geoffroy d'Amboise.

 Bourgogne, Place de l'Abbaye.

The Charollais and the Brion-
nais

The Charollais, separated from the
Mâconnais by the Grosne valley, is part
of the heartland of Burgundy. In the
Middle Ages a proud family held sway in
the castle of Charolles, and the 'Grand
Dukes' later allowed their eldest sons to
bear the title duke of Charollais. We are
more familiar with the name as it
appears on better-class menus: Charollais steaks are renowned, like Bresse
chickens, for their high quality. Nowadays, of course, Charollais cattle are bred
all over the world; but here you can see
them on their home ground. Their light-
dun hide is not very suggestive of the
carnal delights within: only in the evening,
when the descending sun transfigures
everything, does the colour glow against
the dark green of the meadows.

The Brionnais is contiguous with the
western Charollais and extends as far as
the Loire. In the Middle Ages it was one
of the nineteen *bailliages* (bailiwicks –
judicial subdivisions) of the Duchy. Nowadays it is merely a name, appended to
numerous little towns to distinguish
them from other little towns with the
same name in other regions. But it has
an astonishing wealth of churches.

If you must make haste, take the
D980 south from Cluny and then the
busy N79 all the way to Charolles. The
little roads further north have, of course,
more variety to offer. You could, for
example, travel via Donzy-le-National,
where there is a tiny hotel and restaurant, and then Buffières and Sivignon to
Butte de Suin, a lovely vantage-point

with a church and a bar/restaurant. Then you travel down, via Tillay, to La Fourche, just after which you strike the main road to *Charolles* (N79). In Charolles there is an attractive view over the town and its environs from the motte of the former *castle of the dukes of Charollais*. The later *ducal palace* is now the town hall. Charolles is also, of course, a market town: there are regular large sales of livestock.

Paray-le-Monial, with its great *Sacré-Cœur* basilica, is your next port of call. The priory church was built at the same time as *Cluny III* (begun in 1109) and is perhaps the most important of the 'daughters of Cluny'. Because it was not destroyed in the last century – indeed it was carefully restored when the name was changed in 1875 – you can see and study here many of the architectural ideas that in Cluny exist only in drawings. Since the scale of Paray-le-Monial does not approach that of its model, these features look rather more squat than they probably did at Cluny. But that is only the case with the exterior. Inside, you will be amazed by the apparent weightlessness of the vaulting, resting delicately as it does on slim, composite piers. The east end offers the most instructive view from outside, with its succession of diminishing masses: the *ambulatory* rising above the apsides, and above that the *apse* proper, with its pilaster-arcading round the windows, itself backing on to the retaining wall of the *chancel's* pointed tunnel-vaulting. A real textbook example of Romanesque architecture.

Many pilgrims come to Paray-le-Monial. The high point of the ritual year falls on the second Friday after Corpus Christi, a date which goes back to the visions (1673, 1674, 1675) of the nun Marguerite-Marie Alacoque, who was

Sacré-Cœur, Paray-le-Monial

canonised in 1920. Crowds of pilgrims have come each year since 1873 to the *Parc des Chapeleins* and the *Chapelle de la Visitation*. It is partly thanks to their offerings that the church has been so thoroughly restored.

Not far from the church, on the embankment of the placidly flowing Bourbince, is a splendidly theatrical monument to the fallen of the First World War.

You now move on southwards by minor roads via Montceaux-l'Etoile (where there is a church with a fine tympanum over the main doorway) to Anzy-le-Duc.

Anzy-le-Duc's early 11th c. church is of special note. The glowing honey-coloured stone makes it look attractive even from the outside. The octagonal, three-storeyed tower over the crossing, the forceful, harmonious lines of the interior, and the richly ornamented doorways and capitals all help to make

Priory door at Anzy-le-Duc

it one of the most outstanding achievements of its age in ecclesiastical architecture. Note also the doorway in the old priory wall.

Leaving Anzy-le-Duc, drive to Marcigny, and eastwards from there along the D989 to your next stop, Semur-en-Brionnais.

Semur-en-Brionnais was once the capital of the Brionnais, and is the birthplace of Abbot Hugo, the obsessive builder – his father was the *bailli* of the Brionnais. Only the square keep of the old 10th c. *Château de St-Hugues*, where Hugo was born, still stands. A little above the castle, on the highest spot in the town, stands the parish church, a typical Cluniac priory church, as is plain above all from the elevation of the nave: arcades with broken arches, gallery, clerestory. Also of note are the octagonal crossing on three levels and the richly decorated west doorway (Christ in a mandorla, with the Lamb of God above and scenes from the life of St Hilarius underneath), with the same Moorish *alfiz* half-shafts and mouldings as are found at Cluny.

You come finally, via St-Julien-de-Jonzy, to the most southerly point of your excursion, Charlieu.

Charlieu bridges a little river, the Sornin, on an ancient trade-route between the Rhône and the Loire. Its famous *abbey* was founded before Cluny, in 872. But it was not long before it joined the mother-house's powerful outward momentum: it was master masons and craftsmen from Cluny who in the 11th c. built *St-Fortunat*, her 'loveliest daughter' (dedicated 1094). The Revolution razed most of the church to the ground, but you can still see the *narthex*, with the main doorway and the first bay adjoining it, and parts of the *chapter-house* and the *cloister*. Best preserved are the picturesque monastery buildings, especially the *prior's house* (early 16th c.). But Charlieu owes its honourable mention in the art-history books to the magnificent, though damaged, remains of the *three narthex doorways* (in the former west façade and on the north side) with their sculptured tympana, lintels and extrados.

From Charlieu you can drive back to Charolles via either *Varenne-l'Arconce* or *Châteauneuf*, both of which have fine Romanesque churches, and from there along the N79 to either Cluny or Mâcon.

Between Autun and Vézelay: the Morvan

The central region of Burgundy is quite marvellous. If you do not know it, you cannot claim to know Burgundy. That said, a few marginal notes must be entered. When it pleased the centralisers to destroy, by the New Constitution of September 3rd 1791, the historic provinces of France in favour of 83 small administrative *départements* without a past, they divided Burgundy into four units, one up, one down, one left, one right. But their capitals all lay more or less on the edge of Burgundy: Auxerre (Yonne) in the north, Dijon (Côte d'Or) in the east, Mâcon (Saône-et-Loire) in the south, Nevers (Nièvre) in the west. People in the capitals were apparently not interested in the central region of the former province, where the four new departments met. That was the poor old Morvan, which no one actually wanted.

Since no one felt particularly responsible for this region, nothing much happened there: no industrial investment, no urbanisation, no infrastructure for tourism. The centre was undeveloped and so it basically remains today.

The area dealt with in this section is thinly populated, mountainous, covered with forests and pastureland, sometimes austere, sometimes charming. The Morvan measures about 70 km from north to south; its highest point, the *Massif du Bois du Roi* (also called the *Haut-Folin*) reaches an elevation of 902 m. The starting and finishing points of your excursion are the only two 'touristified' spots in the entire region: Autun and Vézelay. It is not particularly easy to find first-rate lodging in the Morvan. Apart from Autun and Vézelay, the only hotels worth mentioning are in Saulieu, roughly half-way between. If you are driving from the east to Autun, the best way is by the D973 from Beaune, a distance of 50 km.

Autun Pop. 22,000

Autun feels like a town entirely unconscious of its proud past and splendid cultural heritage — unassuming, worthy, provincial, sleepy. You catch sight of the tower of the *cathedral of St-Lazare*

Tympanum, St-Lazare, Autun

Lac des Settons, Morvan

while still a good way off; it looms over the houses as though it owned them.

 Augustodunum Aeduorum

Though the Aedui, as long-standing 'brothers of the Roman people', were never forced to abandon their fortress *Bibracte* (Mont Beuvray) (see page 8), in the long run the attractions of the valley and of Roman civilisation proved too alluring. The point of settlement was the Roman fort on the crossing of the River Arroux, 30 km east of Bibracte. It stood at the meeting point of three important military highways, from Chalon-sur-Saône, from Paris and from Tours. Like many of the new Gallo-Roman towns, it began as an administrative centre and, as it attracted settlers, gradually acquired a commercial and artisanal life of its own. Unlike them, it boasted its own walls, probably inherited from the army. The new settlement was patronised by the Emperor Augustus and was permitted to call itself *Augustodunum*. By the early 1st c. AD, as the capital of the *civitas* of the Aedui, the town had built its own theatre and amphitheatre. In the 4th c. it possessed its own rhetorical school. But, despite its walls (6 km long and studded with towers), the town was repeatedly sacked and destroyed by invading German tribes.

The diocese, one of the oldest in Gaul, preserved until the Revolution the name 'bishopric of the Aedui'. Because of its prestige as a former Roman capital, Autun possessed several abbeys, including *St-Martin*, which managed to retain its independence of Cluny. But things really looked up after AD 1079, when the relics of St Lazarus (according to tradition, the first bishop of Marseille, who introduced Christianity into Provence) arrived in Autun, requiring a monumental shrine to do them honour. The church of *St-Lazare* was largely complete by 1146, and rapidly became an important pilgrimage centre, since this Lazarus was not clearly distinguishable from the Lazarus brought back from the dead by Jesus. Autun became a sort of Lourdes for lepers. And with pilgrims came money.

 St-Lazare

Much of the church is in fact not Romanesque but later: the raised roof of the chancel is Gothic; the tower over the crossing and the lateral chapels of the nave-aisles were added by Bishop Rolin (late 15th c.); the two towers of the west façade are actually 19th c. imitations of Paray-le-Monial. But the building as a whole is Cluniac Romanesque, with the usual triple elevation of ground-level arcades (nave and two aisles) with broken arches, blind gallery and clerestory (round-arched windows); composite piers; broken transverse arches; and broken tunnel-vault roof. And, of course, there is the famous *façade*, with its extraordinary tympanum above the main doorway, with the name of its sculptor, Ghislebert, very unusually for his time, inserted beneath Christ's feet: *Ghislebertus hoc fecit* (Ghislebert made this). Several of the capitals almost certainly are also by him, and no scholar doubts that Ghislebert is one of the most important early medieval artist-craftsmen.

In the centre of the *tympanum* is the dominant figure of Christ in a mandorla borne by four angels. On the lintel below him stands an angel with a sword separating the elect, emerging from their graves on the left, from the damned on the right. In the top register is Paradise, with Mary sitting at Christ's right hand, and (probably) Peter and Paul on the other side. In the right-hand section of the central panel you can see a soul being weighed by St Michael and a devil, another devil tearing at the damned, and, in the extreme corner in front of the angel blowing the Last Trump, the entrance to Hell. In the left-hand section appear the Apostles and the elect entering Paradise.

Here we must be content to provide a bare summary description. You should consult the specialist literature for an art-historical evaluation of the importance of this masterpiece and its significance in the history of Romanesque sculpture in Burgundy and France as a whole. But even if you have no specialist knowledge, you can see, in addition to the almost perfect technical skill, that a profound religious feeling has here found artistic expression. The same is true of the capitals of the nave, some of which have especially striking subjects: (r.) Simon the Magus being hurled headlong from heaven; the stoning of St Stephen; the building of Noah's ark; (l.) Christ appearing to Mary Magdalene; Christ's second temptation by Satan; the Nativity.

The capitals, being so high up, are difficult to see properly even with binoculars. But the best examples are on show at eye-level in the *chapter-house*, accessible through the right aisle of the chancel: the flight to Egypt; the dream of the Magi; the adoration of the Magi (Joseph shyly hiding away!); the suicide of Judas Iscariot.

The Musée Rolin lies obliquely across from the church, in a building put up by Cardinal Rolin, the son of Nicolas, and enlarged in the last century. Of all its treasures, you are likely to be most captivated by the erotic suggestiveness of Ghislebert's seductive Eve, taken from the side-door of the chancel in the

18th c. The museum also contains statues (Martha, Mary Magdalene, St Andrew); all that survives of the magnificent mausoleum of St Lazarus (constructed after 1170, demolished in the 18th c. when the chancel was modernised); a selection of Romanesque sculptures from monasteries in Autun; a Madonna and St Catherine that are among the finest Burgundian sculptures of the 15th c.; and a painting of the Nativity by the Master of Moulins (c. 1480).

Gallo-Roman Autun

Apart from the above treasures, the town has little to offer that cannot be paralleled in many another town in France. Among the reminders of its Gallo-Roman past are the remains of the *theatre*, which with seating for 15,000 spectators was the largest in Gaul; two *city gates*, namely the proud *Porte St-André*, still in excellent condition, and the *Porte d'Arroux*; and, just outside the Roman city, the so-called *Temple of Janus*, a massive square edifice that is probably the central chamber (*cella*) of a temple dedicated to (Gallic) Mars.

If you walk from the middle of town round the Champ de Mars, with the

Roman theatre, Autun

splendid wrought-iron railings of the Lycée Bonaparte, and up the hill to the cathedral, you will pass many fine 18th c. houses.

 St-Louis et de la Poste, 6 Rue de l'Arbalète.

 Hostellerie Vieux Moulin, Porte d'Arroux.

 Château de Sully and Mont Beuvray

The Château de Sully, which lies 15 km north-east of Autun, is reached on the D973 (direction Beaune); you turn left at Creusefond (signposted). It is one of the loveliest houses in Burgundy, but alas the interior cannot be visited. All the same, the trip is worth while, especially in the morning, when the mist hangs over the Drée valley and casts a spell over the tranquil countryside.

The oldest sections of the castle go back to the 12th c., but in its present shape it is a typical 16th c. Renaissance building, with four wings and four rectangular corner-towers enclosing an inner courtyard. On the north side, which has been given an 18th c. appearance, there is a monumental staircase leading up to a terrace. The large park (to which one can gain admission) is quite beautiful; and there are numerous outbuildings.

Marie Edmé Patrice Maurice MacMahon, later Marshal of France and Duke of Magenta (1808–93), was born at Sully of an originally Irish Jacobite family. Victor of the Battle of Magenta (1859) against the Austrians in Italy, but captured by the Prussians at Sédan (1870), he was responsible for suppressing the Paris Commune in 1871. Finally he became President of France (1873–9).

Mont Beuvray lies 30 km south-west of Autun and is reached by following the N81, then the D61, D3 and D274. Students of Latin who had to plough through Caesar's *De Bello Gallico* will have met Mont Beuvray under the name *Bibracte*, chief town and refuge of the Aedui. It became famous as the place where in 52 BC Caesar's most dangerous opponent in Gaul, Vercingetorix, induced the leaders of the Gallic tribes to unite in a common struggle against the Roman invaders (see page 8).

You can drive up to the car-park on the levelled summit. There is a footpath, signposted *'Remparts'*, round the earthworks that protected the plateau.

Through the Morvan to Vézelay

If you only want to get from Autun to Vézelay as quickly as possible, a distance of about 80 km, there are good main roads without much traffic (D980 to Saulieu, N6, D957 via Avallon) which will take you there in about two hours. But you may also like to spend up to a whole day getting there, and not be bored for a minute. The Morvan is a thinly populated highland area, reminiscent variously of the Black Forest, the Jura and the Black Mountains. The dominant impression is of an almost timeless remoteness, almost a vacuum in the very heart of France.

In the Morvan there have been no shrines dedicated, no dynasties founded, no battles fought, no wealth amassed. It was the home of poor peasants, woodcutters, charcoal burners, glass-blowers and raftsmen – and of wet-nurses, who gave suck to the newborn children of well-off Parisian families even as late as the last century. With such folk there was not much to be done, and in the rest of Burgundy, for example in the rich Côte d'Or, it was

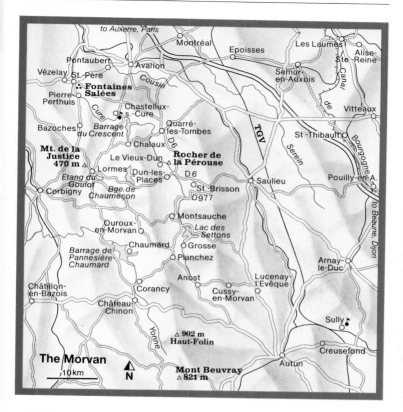

said of them: 'Morvan stock are as grim as the Morvan winds.'

The word Morvan is of Celtic origin and means 'black mountain', which suggests what sort of place it was when it consisted largely of bog and forest – cold and inhospitable. But most of the bogs have now been drained and great areas of forest cleared to create pasture. It rains a good deal, but that, as everyone knows, has its good side. Nowadays great herds of Charollais cattle graze the lush meadows, between which are stretches of splendid deciduous woods, with an amazing variety of

species (beech, oak, chestnut, maple, acacia, lime, ash), a far cry from the dreary monoculture of many recently planted forests.

Woods and water are the only things the Morvan possesses in plenty. The Yonne rises here and flows north, fed by numerous tributaries, debouching eventually into the Seine. But even when it has not travelled far from its source, the volume of water is so great that it became necessary to dam it (the biggest lake is the *Barrage de Pannesière-Chaumard*) so as to ensure a regular flow and the passage of rafts down to Paris. (During the last century the Morvan was the chief source of timber for the building boom when Paris grew so fast, though wooden rafts have not gone down the Yonne for many a year.) But the artificial lakes of the Morvan — of which perhaps the *Lac des Settons* is the loveliest — still govern the water-level in the reservoirs of Paris.

On the Michelin 1:200,000 road-map, the Morvan is distinctive because of the great number of its roads edged with green, which means 'attractive scenery'. But in fact plenty of roads in the Morvan without green edges are just as attractive.

Suggested route: Leave Autun northwards on the D980 as far as Lucenay-l'Evêque. Turn left here to Cussy-en-Morvan and Anost (D88), where you turn right for Planchez (D2, D17). From here drive north (direction Montsauche) via Grosse to the east bank of the *Lac des Settons*.

The lake, created by the damming of the Cure, was constructed as early as 1861. It has now developed into a popular place for watersports. There are no bathing restrictions.

The route continues along the north bank of the lake to Montsauche and from here along the D977*bis* towards St-Brisson. *En route* you pass a pretty little waterfall on the Cure.

Signposts on the road near here mention the *Maison du Parc*. The Morvan has actually been a National Park since 1970. The Maison, which does in fact stand very attractively in an actual park on a small lake, is an information centre for the National Park.

Continue on the D977*bis* to Saulieu.

Saulieu (pop. 3,200) calls itself the East Gate of the Morvan. In the days of the stage-coach, when Saulieu stood on the turnpike road from Paris to Lyon, it was an important staging post, as the number of hotels on the main road (N6) recalls. Since then the motorway has taken away the through traffic, and nowadays the only people who stop in Saulieu do so for one of two reasons: to eat at one of the most famous restaurants in France (the *Côte d'Or*), or to look at the capitals of the basilica of *St-Andoche*.

The church was built early in the 12th c. in place of an 8th c. abbey, and was dedicated to three saints who were martyred here in AD 177. It was repeatedly damaged and rather gives the impression of having been patched up. The sculpted capitals, which rank high in the annals of Burgundian art, are all the more impressive. 'Scholars are now agreed that Saulieu represents the further development of the capitals of the nave at Autun, with a greater sense of three-dimensionality and more graphic narrative style' (Klaus Bussmann). The subjects of the capitals include: the temptation of Christ; Baalam and the ass; the flight to Egypt; the angel barring the way with his sword; and the suicide of Judas Iscariot. One is particularly struck by the extraordinary plasticity of the forms.

From Saulieu, go back a little way (10.5 km) on the D977*bis*, then turn right on to the D6 past St-Brisson and through the lovely forest of *Breuil-Chenue*. On the left you pass a 'dolmen' (signposted). There is hereabouts also a paddock with chamois. Go on through Dun-les-Places, where the road becomes narrower (restrictions), to the hamlet of Le Vieux-Dun. At the bridge over the Cure here, a forest road branches off through the *Forêt au Duc*.

here is a place to park on this road, om which you can climb up the *Rocher 'e la Pérouse* (609 m) to obtain an xcellent view of the Cure valley and the iilly, wooded countryside.

If you wish to enjoy the experience of magnificent woodland to the full, stay on the forest road, which first doubles back (one-way system) and then bears north to Quarré-les-Tombes.

Quarré-les-Tombes, which is on a plateau, owes its name to the discovery of a mysterious cache of around 2,000 sarcophagi near the church. The best explanation for their existence (rather more than a hundred still survive) is that the Merovingian (Frankish) and Carolingian sarcophagus-workshop known to have existed at Chastenay, north of Vézelay, laid out commissions in the surrounding area.

It is only 19 km from Quarré-les-Tombes to Avallon via the D10. If you do not mind getting there more slowly driving on narrow, winding roads, take the D128 westwards from Quarré, turning north at Chaleux to the artificial lake *Barrage du Crescent*. Thence follow the D944 to *Chastellux-sur-Cure*, where you have a view from the bridge of the castle, which for a thousand years has been in the possession of the Chastellux family (no admission). Continue to Avallon.

Avallon Pop. 9,000

The town stands on a granite outcrop high above the Cousin valley, on the northern edge of the Morvan. During the Middle Ages, it was one of the keys to the Morvan, often fought over and as often fortified. In a later age the *fortifications* were turned into little parks and squares, where, beneath the shady trees, you may stroll, ponder or gaze down into the valley over the old walls.

 Tour of Avallon

The best way of getting to know Avallon is to start from the Place Vauban and cross the Place Général de Gaulle, then go along the Grande Rue Aristide Briand to the *Tour de l'Horloge* (clock-tower). The tower, erected in 1465, used to be the watch-tower and is now the emblem of Avallon; the street, paved with cobbles, is lined with mansions, some in rather poor repair: note especially the *Hôtel de Domecy*, which, with its oriels and prominent steps, is typical of 15th c. domestic architecture in Burgundy.

The church of St-Lazare in Avallon, like that at Autun, owes its origins to the cult of St Lazarus, patron saint of lepers, of whom there were so many in the Middle Ages. His head was supposed to be preserved here. The church was dedicated in 1106 as a centre of pilgrimage and later several times extended westwards (the ground falls steeply away to the east). But it has suffered serious damage over the centuries – from war, fire, collapse of the north tower and finally the Revolution. This is

St-Lazare, Avallon

true also of the main doorway on the otherwise indifferent west façade, built about 1150 and linked by art historians because of its stepped jambs and multiple orders to the doorways of emergent Gothic, for example at St-Denis and Chartres. But it is not necessary to know this to observe that Burgundian Romanesque has once again found here a strikingly expressive plasticity, especially in the sculptures of the mouldings, with their angels, signs of the zodiac and images of the months. When you gaze at the marvellous prophet on the right-hand inmost respond, it is difficult to know whether to regret the dreadful damage or to be glad that this fragment at least has been preserved. On the tympanum of the side-doorway it is still possible to make out the scenes of the adoration of the Magi, the presentation in the Temple and the harrowing of Hell.

As you proceed further, you come to the *Promenade de la Petite Porte*, haunt of the lovers and insomniacs of Avallon; here too is the *Gaujard Tower* (1438). From this point, you can go back along the *Remparts* (old walls), past the *Escharguet Tower* and *Beurdelaine Tower*, and so return to the Place Vauban.

 Hostellerie de la Poste, Place Vauban; *Moulin des Ruats*, a little out of town in the Cousin valley.

Ex **Montréal** is a tiny place on an eminence 12 km north-east of Avallon (D957). It has a picturesque main square with 13th c. emplacements and 15th–16th c. houses. Higher up, the hills flatten out into a plateau, where the palace of the legendary Queen Brunehaut (534–614), daughter of the Visigothic king Athanagild, once stood; but not a stone of it is to be seen.

The little church, which has stood up there since the 12th c., hardly looks as though it has much to offer. But it in fact contains a wonderful surprise: 26 *choir-stalls* with unique 16th c. oak carvings. Most of these represent scenes from the New Testament in a very individual and informal fashion, but the two craftsmen who carved them, the Rigolley brothers, also allowed themselves a few little jokes, such as the two lions fighting over a bone and 'self-portraits' of the brothers carousing and feasting.

From the cemetery behind the church there is a fine view over the Serein valley dotted with hamlets and farmsteads, the Auxois and the mountains of the Morvan.

On the way from Avallon to Vézelay, you first go through the secluded *Cousin valley* to Pontaubert and then along the D957, which is also a pleasant road, via St-Père (which has a luxury hotel, *L'Espérance*) up to Vézelay.

Vézelay Pop. 540

The French say that Vézelay is an *haut lieu* of Burgundy, indeed of France. This expression does not refer simply to its altitude. You could translate it as an 'exalted place': partly because of its lofty position, visible for miles around, but also because of its spiritual, religious aura over the centuries, an aura that extends its calming influence even to our down-to-earth century.

 The epitome of medieval piety

Girart de Roussillon, the hero of a later *chanson de geste*, initially founded a monastery c. 860 in the Cure valley, but it was promptly destroyed by the Normans. For his second attempt, he chose a place higher up that was more easily defensible, and allowed it to be occupied by Benedictine monks. At the same

Vézelay

time that the cult of St Lazarus spread north from southern France – you have seen evidence of it at Autun and Saulieu – the cult of Mary Magdalene also inspired a good deal of fervour. The monks of Vézelay succeeded in acquiring her relics (or in convincing the world that they had acquired them) and thus attracted an ever-increasing stream of pilgrims to their monastery.

Vézelay also at about the same time became one of the great assembly points for German pilgrims to Santiago de Compostela, and the monastery had to be enlarged so as to be able to receive the throngs. The new church was started in 1096, but burned to the ground in 1120. In an astonishingly short space of time it was rebuilt. The nave and narthex must have been finished around 1150, but the transepts and chancel had to be dismantled after another fire and were only completed (in Gothic style) c. 1215.

On Easter Sunday 1146, when the narthex must have been still under scaffolding, the basilica of Vézelay had its moment of fame on the world's stage, for it was here that, as papal envoy, Bernard of Clairvaux, full of faith, fanatical and fiery, proclaimed the Second Crusade (1147–9) in response to the Arab conquest of Edessa in 1144. It is said that a hundred thousand pilgrims – at any rate a great number – crowded in and around the church to hear him, including King Louis VII of France and his Queen, Eleanor of Aquitaine. Thou-

sands spontaneously 'took the Cross' and set out for the Holy Land. Though the whole enterprise, fatally split between the German forces under the Hohenstaufen Emperor Conrad III and the French under Louis, ended in total disaster, the church at Vézelay still stands as a symbol of medieval piety and Christian valour.

The basilica of Ste-Madeleine

Visitors to the basilica of *Ste-Madeleine* have to leave their cars in the car-park lower down (Place du Champ-de-Foire) and ascend to the church on foot. Passing through the little town up to the doors of the mighty church, you can imagine yourself in the position of the pilgrims who had reached their goal after all their weary efforts.

The *façade*, in its original form, was completed around 1150; the Gothic porch was put up in the 13th c. Parts of the façade were restored last century by Viollet-le-Duc. Enter the church by the side-door on the right, straight into the narthex.

The *narthex* was dedicated in 1150, later than the nave. Despite its extraordinary size, however, it is only an area for entering and waiting, before stepping into the 'actual' church. This purpose is best grasped as you look from the darkness of the narthex through the main doorway up the bright nave, with all its promise of salvation, to the chancel.

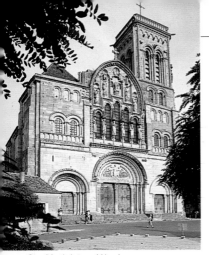

Ste-Madeleine, Vézelay

The *tympanum* of the main door represents Christ in Glory surrounded by the Apostles whom he has charged to bear the Word throughout all the world. The peoples of the world are represented on the lintel and the extrados. The labours of the months and the signs of the zodiac figure in the roundels of the moulding above the extrados. On the tympanum of the side-door on the right (south) you can see scenes from the early life of Christ (including the Nativity), and on the left (north) the encounters with the Risen Christ. Before the Revolution, there was a grand tympanum above the porch depicting the Last Judgement.

The dimensions of the *nave* are also impressive (62 m long), but it mainly derives its effect from the perfect harmony of its proportions and the bright warmth of the interior, produced by the flood of light and the shifting colours of the soft limestone. The nave and aisles are groin-vaulted, with massive round transverse arches painted in red and white. The transition between the Romanesque nave and the Gothic chancel is also achieved with extraordinary sensitivity: the chancel is a bright, radiant space that one may well imagine inspiring a medieval believer with a foretaste of eternal life in the hereafter.

The *nave capitals* are not so well thought of by strict art historians as are those at Autun. Such a judgement is to a non-expert quite incomprehensible. You need have no compunction at taking pleasure in the variety of subject matter, in the sculptors' naive enjoyment in telling a story, or in the expressiveness of the forms they invented for their lyrical, dramatic — indeed graphic — images. There have been many attempts at explaining the subject of one capital in particular, the *mystic mill*, which is on the right of the nave (central pier). Most probably it is a symbolic representation of the relation between the Old and New Testaments: a prophet is grinding corn in a hand-mill, and the Apostle Paul gathers up the meal.

The entrance to the *crypt* is from the south transept. This is Carolingian in origin, extensively altered after a fire in 1165. In the Middle Ages this is where the 'grave' of St Mary Magdalene was situated; some of her relics are still on show there now. The *chapter-house* abuts the same transept; it was constructed towards the end of the 12th c. and restored last century by Viollet-le-Duc. He also restored the sole remaining gallery of the *cloister*. The *well* is also original.

The entrance to the top of the *tower* is by the staircase (200 steps) to the left of the façade. And to finish, you should take one last turn round the outside of the basilica anticlockwise. There is a magnificent view from the terrace at the east end, where the monastery once stood, right over the Cure valley and the Morvan hills.

Rather than return to the Place du

Champ-de-Foire by the same route, you may also stroll back along the walls, while reflecting on the fact that in the 13th c. Vézelay probably had over 10,000 inhabitants; now its population is 540.

 Poste et Lion d'Or, Place du Champ-de-Foire.

 Le Pontot, Place du Pontot.

Through the Morvan to Autun

Leave Vézelay the way you entered. As you drive through *St-Père*, just make time for a quick visit to the church of *Notre-Dame*, a fine example of 13th–14th c. Burgundian Gothic. In St-Père, turn southwards on the D958 towards Pierre-Perthuis. 2 km along this road you pass the excavations at *Fontaines Salées*, where archaeologists have found the remains of a mesolithic camp of the Boreal period (6550–3950 BC), an early Hallstattian urn-field cemetery (8th–7th c. BC), and oak well-heads, which suggest a flourishing bathing establishment, long before the Roman period, based on the brackish springs.

When you reach Pierre-Perthuis, you cross the Cure by a modern bridge 30 m above the river as it thunders through a narrow gorge. From the bridge you can take one final look at Vézelay; then go on to *Bazoches*, still on the D958. The great military engineer Sébastien le Prestre de Vauban (1633–1707), who was born near Avallon, is buried in the church at Bazoches. Soon after the village, turn left on to the D42 to the small town of Lormes.

Lormes (pop. 1,500) is one of the largest centres in the Morvan and a popular summer resort although with no

special attractions. People take trips: short trips to see the view from *Mont de la Justice*, or longer trips to the artificial lake *Barrage de Chaumeçon*, which is an unpretentious place for watersports and popular among fishermen.

Drive through Lormes and out of the town to just past a small lake (the *Étang du Goulot*), then turn left on to the D17 as far as Ourroux-en-Morvan. Turn off here to Chaumard on the narrow D12.

The Barrage de Pannesière-Chaumard is fed by the upper reaches of the Yonne. It is possible to drive all the way along the banks of the artificial lake, with its numerous arms and varied scenery, and to bathe if you wish, as far as the dam at the northern end, which is 50 m high and 340 m long.

You may now take the D944 to Château-Chinon, or keep to the lakeshore and take the longer way round to Chinon, via Corancy.

Château-Chinon (pop. 3,000) is the unofficial 'capital' of the Morvan. It lies below a sheltering bluff with fine views in all directions. The only structures on the bluff now are the three crucifixes of a Calvary, but once the Gauls had a settlement, the Romans a camp and a medieval lord his castle here. It takes about half an hour to walk round the Calvary Hill and take in the views up the Yonne valley. (Start from the Square d'Aligre.)

From Château-Chinon you may drive back to Autun via Mont Beuvray (see page 72) or directly on the D978. Depending on which way you choose, the *Haut-Folin* (*Bois du Roi*), the highest point (902 m) of the Morvan and a moderately good place to ski, will be either on your left or on your right.

Auxerre

The north-west: Lower Burgundy

Lower Burgundy (*Basse-Bourgogne*) cannot offer attractions to compare with the Côte d'Or, Cluny, Autun or Vézelay. You will, of course, find here Romanesque churches and wine, the twin symbols of Burgundy, but they are in more abundance and of greater renown elsewhere in the region. Nevertheless, if you decide you can safely ignore Lower Burgundy, you will miss a great deal that is of interest.

Auxerre Pop. 41,000

The town lies in the middle of north-west Burgundy and the department of the Yonne, of which it is the capital. It may serve as a convenient base for excursions into the surrounding area. Old Auxerre is built in an elevated position overlooking the Yonne: the best views of it are from the right bank of that river. The best way of becoming acquainted with the town is to walk along the Quai St-Marien and the Rue St-Martin between the Pont Paul Bert and the Pont de la Tournelle. The city walls have been pulled down and replaced by a ring road that goes right round the outside of the Old Town. If you insist on driving into the Old Town, you will have to come to grips with a confusing one-

way system. It is better to park your car just outside – that way you will reach the centre at least as quickly and without getting lost.

Three churches and the oldest frescos in France

The centre of town is the *Place Général Leclerc*. This area has fortunately been declared a pedestrian zone. The narrow streets are lined with picturesque half-timbered houses, which have recently been painstakingly cleaned of the plaster that covered them. The *Tour de l'Horloge* (clock-tower) stands on the site of a Gallo-Roman fortification. The tower itself was the *beffroi* (curfew-tower), the emblem of the grant by the dukes of Burgundy of free status to the town. The clock-face on the west side shows the hours, that on the east the movements of the sun and moon.

Proceed via the Place de l'Hôtel de Ville, the Place des Cordeliers and the short Rue Fourier to the cathedral.

The massive bulk of the cathedral of *St-Etienne* dominates the skyline. It is the fifth church to stand on this spot: the earliest allegedly goes back to AD 400, when Auxerre was already a bishopric. In its present form, the cathedral was constructed between 1215 and 1560, and is a sort of synopsis of the development of French Gothic.

The *façade* is 15th c. Flamboyant work, too richly ornamented all the way up to the top of the sole tower: as with many better-known French churches, there was no more money and the builders had to settle for one. Much of the ornamental sculpture was lost during the Huguenot wars in the 16th c: the Huguenots were in no two minds about such 'devilish images'.

In the *tympanum* of the central doorway is a representation of the Last Judgement; above the north doorway, scenes from the life of the Virgin; above the south, scenes from the lives of Christ and John the Baptist. The southern side-doorway is dedicated to St Etienne (St Stephen), the northern to St Germain, the patron saint of Auxerre. The interior is overwhelmingly pure Gothic, Burgundian Gothic in the chancel (1215–c.1250). This latter is probably the airiest and most elegant of all northern French 13th c. chancels.

After the building of the chancel came a break, during which the lower part of the façade alone was worked on. The nave was built only towards the end of the 14th c., and vaulted in the following century. Yet the eye discerns no stylistic discontinuity: the three-storeyed

In the Old Town of Auxerre

elevation is carried throughout, and the combination of minutely judged plasticity of individual parts with the transparency of the walls creates the impression of a totally unified space – airy and light. There is a mass of marvellous 13th c. stained glass in the *ambulatory* that has managed to survive – after the glass of Chartres and Bourges, the best in France of its date. There are scenes from the Old Testament and from the lives of various saints.

The *crypt* is all that remains of the earlier Romanesque church (1057). A number of early frescos (c. 1100) were discovered on the vaults, the most impressive of which is also unique in Christian iconography: Christ riding a white steed, surrounded by four mounted angels (the four horsemen of the Apocalypse: Revelation 6:1–7).

It is just a few minutes' walk from St-Etienne through the narrow alleyways of the oldest part of Auxerre, *La Marine*, to the abbey church, also Gothic, in the north-east of the town.

The abbey church of *St-Germain* dates from the 13th to 15th c. The destruction of the western bays of the nave during the last century has left the lovely Romanesque north tower quite isolated and forlorn in front of the church. Of greater interest in St-

Germain however is the *crypt*, built round the grave of St Germain, whose body was brought from Ravenna early in the 5th c. The groin-vaulted main crypt (841–56) is the most important surviving Carolingian complex in France. In 1927 were discovered here the earliest frescos in the entire country, scenes in typical reds and ochres from the (mostly apocryphal) life of St Stephen, portraits of two bishops of Auxerre and an adoration of the Magi. This part of the crypt leads eastwards through a hall into a Gothic decagonal rotunda with rib-vaulting, the *chapel of St Maximus*, which had to be built in place of an earlier structure because of the weight of the present chancel.

Services are no longer held in the church, which, with its associated Baroque monastery buildings, is due to become a municipal museum.

The last of the three churches that give Auxerre its unmistakable silhouette is *St-Pierre-en-Vallée*. This classic Renaissance building of the 16th–17th c. looks a little odd in its Gothic surroundings, especially in relation to its own Late Gothic tower.

 Le Maxime, 2 Quai de la Marine; *Normandie*, 41 Bd Vauban.

 La petite Auberge, 6 km south in Vaux.

East of Auxerre

Here is a suggested excursion of around 140 km: an interesting day-trip with lots to see.

Leaving Auxerre on the N77 (northern industrial area), it takes rather more than a quarter of an hour to reach Pontigny.

Pontigny has a massive Cistercian church. The abbey here, the 'second daughter of Cîteaux', was founded on the bank of the Serein early in the 12th c.; the church in its present form (*II-III*) was built 1150–90. Its size – it is almost as big as Notre-Dame in Paris – is impressive: 117 m long, 52 m wide at the transepts. In style it represents the second generation of Cistercian churches after the death of Bernard of Clairvaux and is an important document in the transition to Gothic forms. The plain rectangular chancel-oratory of the first church, *Pontigny I* (after 1114), was elaborated in *Pontigny II* (1150) by the addition of several radial chapels, and in *Pontigny III* (c. 1185, modelled on *Clairvaux III*) replaced by a semicircular chancel apse with ambulatory and eleven radial chapels, the spatial forms of which are Gothic. Though the walls and cruciform piers of the nave and crossing (*Pontigny II*) remain firmly Romanesque, the ribbed vaulting over pointed arches (c. 1160) seems also to allude to the new Gothic style as it was first developed around 1140 in the rebuilding of the abbey church of St-Denis near Paris. But the simple, stark ground-plan, the two-level elevation with ground-floor arcade and clerestory, and the rejection of decorative but distracting details such as sculpted capitals and stained-glass windows – all these remain faithful to Bernard's principles. The old abbey buildings, which occupied the area to the north of the church, were used in the last century by the surrounding villages as a source of building stone.

Leave Pontigny on the D91 (south), parallel to the course of the Serein, and drive to Chablis.

Chablis is the home of a world-famous wine. The village has an air of uncommon dullness and generally, apart from the two hours round lunch-time, gives the impression of being deserted. All that matters here is work in the vineyard; and the money that is its fruit has left no visible trace. (It is said that in Chablis people still prefer to put their money in a sock rather than in the bank.)

But even here there is one idyllic spot, the *Promenade du Pâtis* on the bank of the Serein, where the anglers try their luck in the shade of the poplars. The former collegiate church of *St-Martin*, dating originally from the 12th c., has Gothic additions, including the south doorway, which carries ninety-six horseshoes dedicated by pilgrims to the shrine of St Martin.

Chablis is made from the Chardonnay grape; the best vineyards lie on the slopes of the right bank of the Serein facing south-east and south-west to escape frost — the area has constant problems with frost and lack of sun. All seven of the Grand Cru *climats* cluster on the great hill immediately across from Chablis itself. Because of fluctu-

ating production, the Grands and Premiers Crus are extremely expensive — some experts would say the Premiers Crus especially are often over-priced. But with oysters or *andouillettes*, what else can one drink but Chablis?

Off now along the D965, a climbing road with good views of Chablis from the rear window, to your next stop, the handsome little town of Tonnerre.

Tonnerre on the Armançon has an *Ancien Hôpital* (medieval hospice) founded in 1293 by Margaret of Burgundy, Queen of Naples and Sicily, which, together with that of Angers, is the finest such building in France. As in Rolin's hospice in Beaune, which imitates Tonnerre, the great sickroom is combined with a chapel. The original dimensions (91 m by 18 m), with space for forty beds, are astonishing; lovely too is the oak tunnel-vault roof-truss. The finest individual item is the *Entombment*

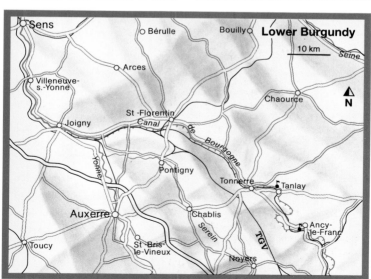

of Christ (1454) by the brothers de la Sonnette, one of the very best examples of 15th c. Burgundian sculpture.

Higher up, the church of *St-Pierre*, largely rebuilt after the disastrous fire that destroyed most of the town in the early 16th c., has a terrace with a fine view of the town. Not far away is an artesian fountain, *La Fosse Dionne*, where once the townswomen used to do their laundry.

Out of Tonnerre, take the D965 over the Canal de Bourgogne to the next stop.

Tanlay is a delightful moated house surrounded by an extensive park with magnificent old trees. The house was begun in 1560 by François d'Andelot, brother of Admiral Coligny, one of the chief Huguenots, but fell foul of the political and military confusion of the Wars of Religion – indeed, it became a secret meeting place of the Huguenot leaders. In 1642 it was sold to Michel Particelli, a royal tax-farmer who had the wherewithal to complete the building on a lavish scale according to new designs by his architect Le Muet. The rich decoration of the interior, quite undamaged by the Revolution, dates from the 17th and 18th c. You can also see the circular tower-room where the Huguenots met (*Tour de la Ligue*), with its Fontainebleau-school *allegorical fresco* celebrating the House of Condé and the Court of Catherine de Médicis.

From Tanlay, take the D118 south until it strikes the D905 and continue south as far as Ancy-le-Franc.

The Château d'Ancy-le-Franc is an important French Renaissance building – it could in fact be on the Loire. For it is an outstanding example of the penetration and spread of Italian artistic tastes in the France of the Italianate

François I (1515–47). The architect Sebastiano Serlio (1475–1554), perhaps the most important of the Italian artists whom François brought to France, built the castle for the Duc de Clermont-Tonnerre. In terms of art history, Ancy-le-Franc marks an important step in the assimilation by France of the Italian Renaissance.

Most visitors will probably respond more positively to Tanlay than to this very cool and severe building. The interior decoration is sumptuous, with everything – wainscoting, ceilings, chimney-breasts, paintings and tapestries – quite exquisite. The portraits in the north-west wing remind one that the Duchesse was the sister of Diane de Poitiers, mistress of Henri II, as clever as she was beautiful.

From Ancy-le-Franc you may either return directly to Auxerre via Chablis (D905, D965) or carry on south to take in Noyers. In either direction the road goes through gently rolling, tranquil farmland with little villages and narrow, winding roads not built for speeding. The only thing that connects this countryside with the great world beyond is the arrow-straight track of the TGV train between Paris and Lyon, which streaks past twice in the hour, filling the air for a few moments with the roar of thunder.

Noyers has only just over 800 inhabitants and is not on the list of 'places one must see'. But here you will find every single thing that makes a little provincial Burgundian town. It is on a slope, protected by the bend of the Serein; its houses are splendid, though perhaps a little in need of repair; the streets are empty; there are flower-pots at the front doors, a simple parish church in late 15th c. Flamboyant, some sections of town wall with towers, a little shop selling old-fashioned postcards....

The Château de Tanlay

Tapestry in the château

Everything is redolent of the past; the future is happening somewhere far away.

Return to Auxerre by way of the D956, a slightly busier road through pleasant, wooded country, via *St-Bris-le-Vineux*, which has lovely medieval houses and a notable Gothic church.

North of Auxerre

Tourists are almost completely unaware of Lower Burgundy north of Auxerre. When they leave the region, they generally take the motorway towards Paris. But one might equally well follow the course of the Yonne by taking the busy N6, and still be able to include one or two things of interest.

Joigny is a lively little town with old city gates, half-timbered houses and two churches, *St-Pierre* and *St-Thibault*, transitional between Late Gothic and Renaissance. In St-Pierre is a charming 14th c. stone *Smiling Madonna*. From the bridge over the Yonne, one has a fine view of the semicircular Old Town.

After Joigny, the N6 passes through a delightful section of the Yonne valley, which separates two forests, the *Forêt d'Othe* to the right and the *Bocage du Gâtinais* to the left.

Villeneuve-sur-Yonne, the next stop, was founded by Louis VII in 1163 and was in the Middle Ages a recognised royal seat. The plan of the well-preserved Old Town has scarcely altered since then. Both the *Porte de Joigny* (south) and the *Porte de Sens* (north) are excellent examples of 13th c. fortification. The round curfew-tower named *Louis-le-Gros* is actually 12th c.; the church of *Notre-Dame* was begun as early as 1163. Pope Alexander III, no less, laid the foundation stone. But after that things slowed down a bit, and the town went on being built until the 16th c.

By the time you reach Sens on the N6, you are no longer really in Burgundy. But, since it is still in the Yonne department, it is included here.

Sens (pop. 28,000) has an interesting history going back to Celtic times. The Senones, one of the most powerful Gallic tribes, settled round here and gave the town their name (its Roman name was Agedincum). It was a branch of the Senones who, under their king, Brennus, invaded Etruria in 390 BC, sacked Rome and put fear into Roman hearts.

In the Middle Ages Sens was a spiritual centre of very considerable importance and the seat of an archbishop who, as primate of Gallia and Germania, was actually the superior of the bishop of Paris. The chancel of the cathedral of *St-Etienne*, which has aisles and an ambulatory that were begun about 1140, is one of the key points in the transition from Romanesque to Gothic, though its influence upon later developments is debated. Among details, note particularly the splendid façade and the surviving stained glass.

The cathedral *treasure* is one of the most magnificent in France. As well as splendid examples of work in gold, ivory and enamel, there is an amazing collection of liturgical vestments and embroidered stuffs, the oldest of which dates from the 5th c. Connected to the cathedral is the *Palais Synodal-Officialité*, a sumptuous 13th c. building now in use as a museum. Here note especially the Gallo-Roman mosaics and the tapestries and sculptures from the cathedral.

There is finally also a *Musée Municipal*, which has interesting archaeological finds from the area and a collection of paintings.

Burgundy on the Loire

It is difficult for the extreme west of the region to make good its claim to be part of Burgundy. The boundaries of the Duchy only reached the Loire further south, in the Charollais. By contrast, the historical county of the Nivernais (duchy from 1538) was only temporarily part of Burgundy and has anyway its own history and dynastic complications. But since the Constitution of 1791 there has been only the department of Nièvre, which is one of the departments that make up the region of Burgundy. So at the end of your visit you might take a short trip along the Loire, following the N7 northwards from Nevers as far as Briare. The direct route to Nevers from Autun is via Château-Chinon by the D978 (103 km).

Nevers Pop. 50,000

By 52 BC its strategic position made Nevers (?Noviodunum Aeduorum, later Nevirnum) a centre of Roman power — indeed, when it was sacked by the insurgents, Caesar lost almost all his personal baggage there. But it was never a *civitas*-capital, and remained of limited importance in Roman times. In the 6th c. it was made a bishopric. Its chief importance lay in its river-traffic: stone and timber were shipped from Nevers to the building sites of the great Loire châteaux. In 1565 the Duchy passed by marriage into the possession of the Gonzaga dukes of Mantua, and from this link with Italy developed (from 1575) the fine faience industry that has made Nevers famous among connoisseurs. By 1650 there were twelve faience factories in the town.

There is a big car-park in the Place Carnot, from where it takes just five minutes to reach the historic city centre, the *Place Ducale*. Here you will find the former *Palais Ducal*, an elegant Late Gothic building with a fine Renaissance staircase-tower, and the *cathedral*, a mixture of Romanesque and Gothic styles interesting mainly for its secondary western chancel — very unusual in France. Not far away, in the Rue St-Genest, is the *Musée Municipal*, with a notable *collection of faience*, said to be the best in France. A little further on again is a splendidly impressive gate-tower, the *Porte du Croux*, a well-preserved fragment of the city walls in an area that was badly bombed in the last war; nowadays it houses an *archaeological museum* with some fine Romanesque sculpture. Over on the other side of the Old Town (south-east) is a lovely Romanesque church, *St-Etienne*, built entirely between 1063 and c.1100 and intact except for the loss of the two west towers and the upper sections of the tower over the crossing.

Nevers

Along the Loire to Briare

Take the N7 north. The road at first is some distance from the river but joins it at La Charité-sur-Loire.

La Charité-sur-Loire should ideally be viewed for the first time from the left bank of the river. It really is a beautiful sight: the Loire, the lovely arcs of the bridges, and then the houses of the Old Town huddled together, their steeply pitched roofs lorded over by the priory church of *Ste-Croix-Notre-Dame*. The church was begun in the mid-11th c. and dedicated in 1107, but altered several times in the 12th c. It was one of the five 'oldest daughters' of Cluny, and, after Cluny III, at one time the largest church in France. As the result of a fire in 1559 that destroyed half the nave, only the façade and the tower remain standing at the west end; the remaining nave was given a completely incongruous Baroque face-lift. But the chancel and the transepts are among the finest examples of Romanesque architecture in Burgundy. The priory itself was destroyed in the Wars of Religion: the Huguenots massacred all the monks and over a thousand Catholics here in 1569.

Pouilly-sur-Loire is also on the N7, 11 km north of La Charité. It produces an excellent white wine (Sauvignon), which, as Pouilly-Fumé, has become increasingly popular abroad over the past few years. But it is counted as a Loire wine, not a white Burgundy: its near relative, Sancerre, grows not far away on the slopes of the left bank of the Loire.

The N7 continues to *Cosne-sur-Loire*, which in the 18th c. was the Woolwich of France, producing fine cannon, muskets and anchors, and to *Briare*, where the *Canal Latéral à la Loire* crosses over the river. The iron *Pont du Canal*, built by Eiffel (see page 25), was in its day a technical marvel: you can still sense the

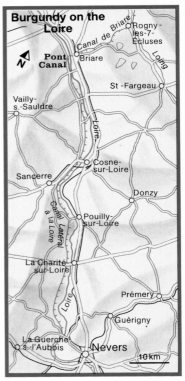

contemporary pride in an outstanding engineering achievement from the cast-iron marine emblems. The object was to link the canal, which ran along the left bank of the Loire, with the 17th c. Canal du Briare that connects the Loing with the Loire. (At *Rogny-les-Sept-Ecluses*, where the Canal du Briare enters the Loing, you can still see the seven locks that are also an extraordinary achievement for their period.)

At Briare, the Loire leaves the department of Nièvre, and Burgundy too. If you wish to continue your trip up the Loire, you are advised to consult the RAC Travel Guide *France: Loire Valley*.

Useful things to know

Before you go
Time to visit
The most popular time to visit Burgundy, as usual with wine country, is autumn. The pulses of tourists and photographers quicken as the vine-leaves colour and the vintage begins. Moreover, the weather at that time of year is generally fairly settled. But because everyone now knows this, autumn is in fact high season in Burgundy. If you have not booked in advance, you will often find the few hotel rooms all taken. You should also avoid the French summer vacation (July and August) and the period from November to March.

The months of May and June are the best time for a trip to Burgundy. The temperatures are then quite mild and any rainfall is light; everything is green or in bloom.

Insurance
You are strongly advised to take out holiday insurance, including cover against medical expenses.

As a member of the EC France has a reciprocal agreement with other EC countries, under which free medical treatment can be obtained for those entitled to it in their own country. To obtain this benefit a UK national has to be in possession of form E111, obtainable from the DSS; an application form is available from the DSS or at main post offices.

Anyone travelling by car should arrange comprehensive insurance cover for the duration of the holiday.

Getting to Burgundy
By sea/road: For British visitors the most convenient ports are Calais, Dunkirk and Boulogne or Le Havre and Dieppe, depending on both your starting point in the UK and the part of Burgundy you are heading for. The same considerations will dictate whether you bypass Paris to the east or west. A glance at the road-map will show that, in either case, you can cover a fair part of the journey by motorway.

By air: All the major international airlines fly to Paris, but there are also airports in Dijon and Lyon. The latter will be particularly useful if you wish to visit Burgundy from Paris or from other French cities. Ask your travel agent for details.

By rail: The Burgundy region is well served by the rail network. Trains to this area from Paris leave from the Gare de Lyon. Information from French Railways (see page 94) and travel agents.

Passport and customs regulations
No visa required by British or US visitors staying under three months. British tourists need a valid standard passport or British Visitor's Passport.

Personal belongings of people entering the country are not subject to duty. These include still and video cameras, tape recorders, portable radios, telescopes and binoculars, portable typewriters and the usual camping equipment. In addition, EC residents may bring in (duty paid) 300 cigarettes (or 75 cigars or 400 g tobacco), 5 litres of wine and 1.5 litres of spirits over 22% (3 litres under 22%).

EC residents may take into or bring back from France duty free 200 cigarettes or 50 cigars or 250 g tobacco, 1 litre of spirits over 22% (2 litres under 22%) and 2 litres of wine.

Non-EC visitors should check allowances with their travel agent.

During your stay

Currency

The monetary unit in France is the French franc (F), equivalent to 100 centimes (c). Currently in circulation are coins up to the value of 10 F as well as banknotes in denominations of 10, 20, 50, 100 and 500 F. Exchange rates are subject to fluctuation and should be checked in the national press or at banks.

There are no restrictions on the import of foreign currency into France. All French banks, bureaux de change and most hotels will cash Eurocheques.

Credit cards are in fairly common use; most hotels, restaurants and petrol stations and many shops will accept the major ones. However, it is safest to carry a supply of cash with you against the possibility of their not being accepted.

Public holidays

January 1st; Easter Monday; May 1st (Labour Day); May 8th (Armistice Day 1945); Ascension Day; Whit Monday; July 14th (Bastille Day); August 15th (Assumption); November 1st (All Saints' Day); November 11th (Armistice Day 1918); December 25th.

Pharmacies and medical assistance

Pharmaceutical chemists' shops have a large green cross outside. You can obtain the name and address of the nearest appropriate doctor and/or casualty hospital from any chemist.

Post

Main post offices (*PTT*) are open all day; smaller ones are open Mon.–Fri. 8 am–noon and 2–6 pm; Sat. 8 am–noon.

Stamps (*timbres*) may also be purchased in tobacconists', bars and bistros, and in hotels.

Telephones

French telephone numbers all have eight digits, composed of the two-digit departmental code and the six-digit subscriber's number. Only when phoning to and from Paris must you still use the old 16 code that used to be universal. You can phone abroad without difficulty from any post office and from most phone boxes, as well as from hotels. First dial the international code (19), wait for the tone and then dial the national code (44 for the UK, 1 for the US and Canada; omit initial 0 from the area code). It is nowadays more and more common even in the provinces to find card-phones. *Télécartes* of various values may be obtained from post offices. International calls are comparatively cheap, but hotels impose a surcharge of around 50%.

Tobacco, cigarettes

People usually buy cigarettes and tobacco in one of the numerous bars that have kiosks inside. Such bars carry a red double-cone sign outside, which is supposed to represent a stylised plug of chewing tobacco. In larger towns there are also specialist shops.

Newspapers

English and American newspapers are to be found only in the centres of large towns, and even then most readily in a *Maison de la Presse*. You can also buy the better-known (serious) papers at large stations and airports, usually one day late.

Transport

It is unfortunately fairly essential to take your car with you to Burgundy or hire one in France: there is plenty of public transport (trains, buses), but the places that are worth visiting are scattered so widely over the region that you would lose far too much time waiting around for connections.

Consult your travel agent for information on car hire.

Opening times

Public offices: To make absolutely sure of being able to see someone, you should call between 9 am and noon. It is never certain that there will be another opening time after the obligatory closing for lunch.

Banks are generally open from 9 am–noon and 2–4 pm. This may not be the case in very small towns. Banks are all shut over the weekend.

Shops: There are standard opening times only for bigger shops in towns: 9.30 am–6.30 pm. Otherwise, be prepared for lunch-time closing, say between 1 and 4 pm. Shops are in that case open later in the evening. Grocers and other food shops (especially bakers) are also open on Sunday mornings, and in consequence generally closed all day Monday.

Museums: Larger museums owned by the State or a local authority are open on Sundays, when they are free. By contrast, privately owned museums are almost all closed on Sundays and holidays. Traditionally, museums in France are closed on Tuesdays, but for practical reasons they are now sometimes closed on Mondays instead.

Churches and religious houses are usually closed from noon–2 pm. (It goes without saying that religious services and sightseeing should not overlap!)

Castles and houses are mostly in private hands and their opening times very variable. Check at the area tourist office (see page 94).

Touring by car

Vehicles travel on the right. Seat belts must be worn at all times. Motorists should carry the following: a nationality plate fixed to the back of the car; a warning triangle (unless car has hazard lights); spare sets of bulbs for all lights.

Priority: The old system, whereby traffic entering a road from the right had priority (*priorité à droite*), no longer applies, traffic on major roads now having priority (as does traffic already on roundabouts). However, signs will occasionally indicate exceptions (for example at some roundabouts) and drivers should familiarise themselves with these signs.

Speed limits: in built-up areas 50 kph (31 mph); outside built-up areas 90 kph (56 mph), but 80 kph (50 mph) in rain; on dual carriageways 110 kph (68 mph), but 100 kph (62 mph) in rain; on motorways 130 kph (81 mph), but 110 kph (68 mph) in rain. Drivers who have held a licence for less than one year: 90 kph maximum.

Documents: In addition to a valid driving licence and vehicle registration certificate it is advisable for motorists to obtain an international 'green card' insurance certificate.

Filling stations in country areas are often few and far between, or so modestly equipped that it is easy to miss them. Many close at lunch-time. Stations selling lead-free petrol (*essence sans plomb*) can be found in most towns and on motorways.

Walking tours

In France the pleasure of physical activity in fresh air and agreeable surroundings is now gradually being recognised, and every year new public footpaths are marked out in Burgundy. Because of its geography, it is particularly possible to combine interesting sightseeing with pleasurable walking or trekking here. Footpaths are generally clearly marked: the long-distance French routes, the 'grandes randonnées', are marked with red and white signs and are very easy to follow. The 'Tour du Morvan par les grands lacs', the grand walk featuring the hills and lakes of the Morvan, goes from one end of central Burgundy to the other (marked in yellow and red). You can buy booklets on these routes in bookshops. Some of the tourist offices can supply information relevant to their areas (see page 94.)

Narrowboats (See also page 25.)

The two centres for renting narrowboats are *Auxerre*, which is linked to the canal system of Burgundy by the Yonne, and *St-Jean-de-Losne*, rather more than 30 km south-east of Dijon (D968), which lies at the meeting point of the Canal de Bourgogne, the Ouche and the Saône. Costs vary with the season. Information from: Bourgogne Voies Navigables, 1/2 Quai de la République, 89000 Auxerre.

Electricity

220 v/50 Hz AC. French sockets do not normally take the standard UK or US plug; a Continental adaptor (obtainable from electrical dealers) will almost certainly be necessary.

Tipping

With few exceptions, service is now included in hotel and restaurant bills (s.c. = *service compris*). But that has not entirely done away with the tip as an acknowledgement or expression of satisfaction. Note that over-generosity is as much a fault as meanness. Taxi-drivers, porters, hairdressers and waiters expect a tip of around 8–10% of the bill.

Festivals and events

January 22nd: Vintage festival of St Vincent, patron saint of wine-growers. On the Saturday following there is a procession in honour of the saint in a different commune on the Côte each year (*Fête tournante*).

February 27th (in Chalon-sur-Saône): International fur-trade exhibition (*Foire froide des Sauvagines*).

February/March (in Chalon-sur-Saône): Carnival week round Ash Wednesday (*Mardi Gras*).

Second half of May (Mâcon): French national wines sale.

May 31st (Semur-en-Auxois): Thoroughbred horse-racing (*Fête de la Bague*).

July 1st–August 10th (in several towns): Nuits de Bourgogne Festival, with concerts, ballet and theatre performances.

Friday after Corpus Christi (Paray-le-Monial): Pilgrimage to *Sacré-Cœur*.

Sunday before or after June 24th (Brancion, Mont St-Vincent): Celtic summer solstice bonfire-night.

July 22nd (Vézelay): Pilgrimage to *Ste-Madeleine*.

Last Sunday in July (Auxerre): Feast of St Germain.

First Sunday in August in uneven years (Charolles): International folk festival.

End of August (Saulieu): Festival and livestock market.

First and second weekend in September (Dijon): Wine festival (*Fête de la Vigne*).

Weekend nearest to September 7th (Alise-Ste-Reine): Pilgrimage to *Ste-Reine*; procession in period costume.

First half of November (Dijon): Gastronomic trade fair.

Third Saturday–Monday in November (Côte d'Or): Wine festival in Clos Vougeot and Meursault (*Les Trois Glorieuses*, see page 48).

Fourth Sunday in November (Chablis): Wine festival.

Son et lumière

This particular form of 'guided tour through history' is not to everyone's taste. But one must allow that it has been brought to a fine degree of professionalism.

Performances take place in the evenings in summer; you can find out dates and times from the tourist offices of the departments. Performances are presented at: Beaune (Hôtel des Ducs de Bourgogne); Bourg-en-Bresse (Eglise de Brou); Semur-en-Auxois (in the Old Town); and Semur-en-Brionnais (Château St-Hugues).

Shopping

In Burgundy there is very little trade in souvenirs of the usual sort. But there is no need on that account to go home empty-handed. In Dijon, of course, connoisseurs buy mustard (specialist shop: *Moutarde Maille*, Rue de la Liberté) and *Crème de Cassis* (blackcurrant liqueur), one of the ingredients of *Kir* (see page 36). If you require something with a slightly longer life, there are plenty of local pottery products, from humble earthenware to the valuable and famous faience of Nevers.

Buying wine

You can make things easy for yourself by simply tasting wine in the vaults of a *négociant* – especially numerous in Beaune – and taking a few bottles with you. In such a case the first consideration is the price, the second the vintage. The risk of being taken for a ride is extremely small. Sharp practice is not common in the wine-trade of Burgundy: official supervision is too strict for that.

Recommended addresses:

Beaune: *L'Ambassade du Vin* (school of wine-tasting): 23 Rue des Tonneliers; *Caves des Cordeliers*, 6 Rue de l'Hôtel-Dieu (in an old Franciscan monastery); *Marché aux Vins*, Rue Nicolas Rolin (old vaulted cellar); *Patriarche*, 7 Rue du Collège (old vaulted cellar); *Caves Exposition Reine Pédauque*, 2 Faubourg St-Nicolas (an exhibition cellar, which sets out the most important wine-growing areas in a very original manner); *Domaine Goud de Beaupuis*, Château des Moutots, Chorey-les-Beaune (between Beaune and Aloxe-Corton: a working *éleveur* in an ancient stately home with park and surrounding vineyards).

Dijon: *Caveau de la Porte Guillaume*, 2 Rue de la Liberté (wine-bar in the cellar of the Hôtel du Nord, off the Place Darcy); *La Cour aux Vins*, 3 Rue Jeannin (wine shop with wine-tasting and discussion).

Gevrey-Chambertin: *Caveau du Syndicat d'Initiative.*

Marsannay-la-Côte: *Cave co-opérative des Grands Vins Rosés*, 21 Rue de Mazy.

Meursault: *Domaine du Château de Meursault*, now owned by Patriarche of Beaune: splendid 14th c. cellar; *Ropiteau Frères*, *négociant* house with some estate wines: former property of the Hospices de Beaune.

Nuits-St-Georges: *Morin Père et Fils*, Quai Fleury (wine vaults with 18th c. oak barrels).

Santenay: *Caves du Château de Philippe le Hardi; Caves Prieur Brunet*, Rue de Narosse (extensive vaults in 15th c. style).

Vougeot: *La Grande Cave*, Route Nationale 74 (fine old vaults).

Besides these, many domains offer wine-tasting and direct sales to the public.

Eating out

It is practically impossible to travel in France without the *Guide Michelin – France*, the annually revised Michelin guide to hotels and restaurants. There simply is no other book with the same breadth of information and reliability. Those with a taste for fine food will, of course, be mainly interested in restaurants with one, two or three stars, the justice of whose allocation is ever heatedly debated.

More fun to read is its newer competitor, the *Gault-Millau*. It mentions far fewer restaurants, but its comments are often quite amusing and its judgements not as schematic as those of the Michelin. Travellers to France who take their eating seriously should really consult both.

Important addresses
Diplomatic offices

British Embassy
35 Rue du Faubourg St-Honoré
75008 Paris; tel. 1 42 66 91 42

US Embassy
2 Av Gabriel
75008 Paris; tel. 1 42 96 12 02

Canadian Embassy
35 Av Montaigne
75008 Paris; tel. 1 47 23 01 01

Australian Embassy
4 Rue Jean Rey
75724 Paris; tel. 1 45 75 62 00

New Zealand Embassy
7 ter Rue Léonard de Vinci
75116 Paris; tel. 1 45 00 24 11

Irish Embassy
4 Rue Rude
75116 Paris; tel. 1 45 00 20 87

Tourist information

In UK
French Government Tourist Office
178 Piccadilly
London WIV OAL; tel. 071 499 6911

French Railways
179 Piccadilly
London W1V 0BA; tel. 071 493 4451

In USA
French Government Tourist Office
610 Fifth Avenue
New York NYC 10021

In France
Comité Régional de Tourisme de Bourgogne
Préfecture, 21041 Dijon Cédex;
tel. 80 55 24 10 or 80 43 81 81

Larger towns and smaller ones with tourist interest have a *Syndicat d'Initiative* (tourist office). Here you will find an abundance of brochures about anything and everything, from tourist routes to restaurants, hotels and festivals, regional museums and nature parks, the town itself, the surrounding area and the whole *département*. Many hotels also keep a supply of tourist information.

RAC

RAC Motoring Services Ltd
RAC House
PO Box 100
South Croydon CR2 6XW;
tel. 081 686 2525

French national motoring organisations

Automobile Club de France
6–8 Place de la Concorde
75008 Paris; tel. 1 42 65 34 70

Association Française des Automobilistes
9 Rue Anatole de la Forge
75017 Paris; tel. 1 42 27 82 00

Useful words and phrases

Although English is fairly widely understood in established tourist areas, the visitor will undoubtedly find a few words and phrases of French very useful.

please	s'il vous plaît
thank you (very much)	merci (bien)
yes/no	oui/non
excuse me	pardon
do you speak English?	parlez-vous anglais?
I do not understand	je ne comprends pas
good morning	bonjour
good evening	bonsoir
good night	bonne nuit
goodbye	au revoir
how much?	combien?
I should like	je voudrais
a room with private bath	une chambre avec bain
the bill, please! (in hotel)	la note, s'il vous plaît
(in restaurant)	l'addition
everything included	tout compris
when?	à quelle heure?
open	ouvert
shut	fermé
where is . . . street?	où se trouve la rue . . . ?
the road to . . . ?	la route de . . . ?
how far is it to . . . ?	quelle est la distance à . . . ?
to the left/right	à gauche/à droite
straight on	tout droit
post office	le bureau de poste
railway station	la gare
town hall	l'hôtel de ville/la mairie
exchange office	le bureau de change
police station	le commissariat/la poste de police
public telephone	la cabine téléphonique
tourist information office	l'office de tourisme/
	le syndicat d'initiative

		0 zéro
		1 un/une
doctor	le médecin	2 deux
chemist	le pharmacien	3 trois
toilet	la toilette	4 quatre
ladies	dames	5 cinq
gentlemen	messieurs	6 six
engaged	occupé	7 sept
free	libre	8 huit
entrance	l'entrée	9 neuf
exit	la sortie	10 dix
today/tomorrow	aujourd'hui/demain	11 onze
Sunday/Monday	dimanche/lundi	12 douze
Tuesday/Wednesday	mardi/mercredi	20 vingt
Thursday/Friday	jeudi/vendredi	50 cinquante
Saturday/holiday	samedi/jeu de congé	100 cent

Index

Original German text: Hans Eckart Rübesamen. Translation: R. Gordon
Series editor, English edition: Jane Rolph

© Verlag Robert Pfützner GmbH, München. Original German edition

© Jarrold Publishing, Norwich, Great Britain 1/91. English language edition worldwide

Published in the US and Canada by Hunter Publishing, Inc.,
300 Raritan Center Parkway, Edison NJ 08818

Illustrations: J. Allan Cash Ltd. pages 1, 3, 6, 52, 71, 80; James Davis Travel Photography pages 56, 75; French Government Tourist Office pages 12, 26, 27, 30, 35, 39; D. Hughes-Gilbey pages 19, 24, 77, 78; E. Greenwood pages 16, 40 (both), 50 (both), 54, 60, 62, 64, 67, 68; R. Moss page 87; U. Snowdon page 85; World Pictures pages 31, 44, 57.

The publishers have made every endeavour to ensure the accuracy of this publication but can accept no responsibility for any errors or omissions. They would, however, appreciate notification of any inaccuracies to correct future editions.

Printed in Italy
ISBN 0–7117–0484–8